MW01128848

The Woman in the Basement

The Woman in the Basement

How to Live Your Best Life 75% of the Time

Tina A. Williams

First paperback edition July 2020

Book design by Krista Kasper
Edited by Lee E. Calaca

ISBN 979-866-418-2972 (paperback)

www.womaninthebasement.com

CONTENTS

AUTHOR'S NOTE

PMDD is a disorder that can affect anyone who menstruates, including some sufferers that do not identify as women. My story, *The Woman in the Basement* is told from my perspective as a woman assigned female at birth. It's not lost on me that my story is one of many. I encourage everyone to join me in educating the world and spreading awareness from different points of view. It is vital to the success and happiness of the next generations to not only speak our truth but scream it from the rooftop for everyone to hear. Because undoubtedly, through our vulnerability we can lift others up and provide hope where it's required.

DISCLAIMER

To be clear, I'm not a medical professional and the information in this book is not a substitution for qualified medical advice. The contents of this book are not intended to diagnose or treat any medical condition. This story includes firsthand accounts of self-medicating with psilocybin mushrooms which are still illegal in many areas. Do your own research and consult qualified legal advice before pursuing any substances mentioned in this book. The author and any affiliates, partners, employees, contractors or business associates expressly disclaim any liability, loss or risk, personal or otherwise, that is incurred as a consequence, directly or indirectly of the use and application of any of the contents of this book. This book is a true story, though I have slightly altered the chronology to protect myself and others.

75% UPTIME

"As the realization crept over me, at how close I had come, I also knew it would only be a month or so before once again, my own womb would try to kill me."

(Suzi Taylor, I Blame the Hormones)

There's a certain calm that can flow through your veins. An addictive peace that transforms your relationship with the world around you. A mental space that allows you to explore the edges of your potential and push past the imaginary boundaries you've placed for yourself. The details you've missed are now center stage and the world appears more vivid and vibrant. Connections become stronger. Your song begins to vibrate at a higher frequency and becomes stable. Your life's work has woven itself into every fiber of your being and is now evident in your thoughts and actions.

From the moment you wake up, it's who you are, it's who you've become, and it's your own defined habit of greatness. Distraction is spotted from a mile away and you begin living in blissful focus. For many, it will take being pushed to their absolute breaking point before ever scratching the surface of their individual human potential. Life on the other side of despair, however, can make up for every negative moment, and our lives can be filled with so much pleasure and purpose that greatness spills over for the rest of the world to enjoy.

For me, finding my true potential and living my best life wasn't a choice; it was necessary for survival. I had to find extreme inner peace, happiness, and extraordinary greatness, and I had to do it fast. Not the run of the mill type of life, not the status quo, but something much better than that. An exceptional reality, living as an exceptional human as often as possible. I required more, a lot more.

In December 2019, I was diagnosed with premenstrual dysphoric disorder, a diagnosis that would prompt me to change my entire life. Around 5% of women live with the debilitating condition known as PMDD. One to two weeks before a period, PMDD sufferers can experience extreme mood swings with depression and anxiety that can disrupt everything about their daily activities including work, social, and home life. It can cause damage to personal and professional relationships and create overwhelming feelings of hopelessness. Suicidal thoughts are common.

According to the International Association for Premenstrual Disorders, roughly 30% of women with PMDD attempt suicide.[1] The cause is unknown, and the treatment varies from patient to patient.

It would be a grueling test of my inner strength and resilience one week out of every month. This would equate to roughly 25% of my childbearing years being absolutely miserable. Every month when my brain tells me to drive my car over a bridge, I have to pull myself back, and I require a valid reason— every single time.

The reason to save myself must be much stronger than the extreme panic attacks and severe suicidal depression that would plague me.

I had to find my purpose, my calling, and truly live it. I had to relish in the bliss of a purpose-driven life that would pull me back from my own self-sabotage. My life had to be so damn good that even I am jealous of it when my disorder hijacks my thoughts. The inner battle still plays out every month, but I always win. Self-development has never been a choice, it's my mission, my passion, and my life saver. My mode of living went from a ball of tears clinging to the bathroom floor to an accomplished author in a matter of months. I went from a person who couldn't stand to live, to someone who has countless reasons *not* to die.

Getting there certainly wasn't pretty. Throughout my journey, I would look in the mirror and find a teary-eyed mad scientist type on a mission. She wasn't always put together, but she was always smart. She was quiet and observant, never showing her true colors and ideas to the world, a true introvert who found peace in total isolation, deep in her own thoughts. She removed herself from the world as much as possible, guarding herself from a cruel place that didn't understand her out-of-the-box thinking and unconventional ways.

Her challenge of the status quo and social norms would drive her to isolation as she struggled to have a conversation with just about every person she met. She would bury herself in work to make up for her shortcomings and work throughout the night to avoid her own family. She would go to great lengths to hide her emotions from the rest of the world, even if it meant taking multiple trips to cry in the bathroom at work. She would always be prepared to fix her makeup and fabricate stories of allergies to account for her puffy teary eyes. She was always hiding, always running, always doing, always learning, but never living.

This mad scientist I saw in the mirror was a talented systems analyst with black frame glasses and long brown hair who stuck out like a sore thumb in board rooms full of alpha males. Surrounded by talented engineers, architects, and software developers, she took every opportunity to learn something new. In the process of running from herself, she switched jobs often, learning even more with each move. Her ability to solve problems was rooted in her out of the box thinking and desire to learn. When she wasn't crying in the bathroom, she was a force to be reckoned with and everyone around her knew it.

She would move up in each company just in time to leave. She would save face by avoiding higher stress environments and decline promotions that she deserved.

She was nothing short of amazing—75% of the time.

She would run in her hamster wheel of hell for years before finally spiraling out of control and coming to terms with the fact that she was a brilliant, hot, fucking mess.

My life was on the line and I knew it. I wanted to die every month like clockwork. I needed to figure something out and I needed it to happen quickly. I was recommended treatments consisting of trying something for 3 months to see if it worked before trying something new. That would equate to 3 full weeks of hell before starting a different treatment and hopefully finding something that fixed me along the way. Thankfully, I happened to be the problem solver type, at least 75% of the time. I needed a mechanism to manage my new way of life, a new approach to living.

If I couldn't fix my 25%, I decided I wouldn't waste even one moment of my 75%.

I needed my good days to be extraordinary to make up for the week of hell that I would experience every month. Living up to my fullest potential 75% of the time would produce a better result than spending 100% of my life spinning my wheels and feeling sorry for myself. I wouldn't stop fighting my PMDD,

5

but I would stop allowing it to control 100% of my time. I believe the concept of living a great life most of the time is an attainable goal for everyone, including sufferers of PMDD.

Everyone has bad days, and humans are allowed to suffer sometimes; it's part of who we are and, unfortunately, we can't grow without it. Imagine a world full of people living as their truest self, 75% of the time. Imagine a world full of people exploring every inch of their greatness for most of their life. The darkness will always exist in every single one of us, no matter how pulled together we are. We will fail, we will doubt ourselves, and we will inherently struggle to find true happiness. But it's what we do with the rest of our time that truly matters. The other side of suffering is where we need to shine the light and explore who we are as individuals.

I read several self-help books to formulate a strategy for living my best life outside of PMDD, but nothing really hit the spot. I needed something vastly different. My goal wasn't to become rich or build the perfect relationship, my goal was to be the absolute best version of that woman sitting in the bathroom at work crying. She deserved a system for being unwell 25% of the time so that she could focus on being brilliant for the other 75%.

The ideas had to come from a depressed, female, mad scientist who got locked in a room for a few months and came up with an interesting method to unfuck her own life. The author needed to be an emotionally disturbed train wreck with a sprinkling of self-destructive behavior. And the setting was going to be America, 2020, hell year, a year of massive change for the nation and the world. The story needed to include a series of epic failures and self-medicating. I couldn't find the book I was looking for, so I decided to write it instead.

THE PSILOCYBIN LOGIN

"Being human is a condition that requires a little anesthesia."

(Freddie Mercury)

Like so many others who struggle through the human condition, I spent most of my life blurring reality with a variety of mind-altering substances. As the world around me bubbled over with never-ending information that needed to be processed, I searched for methods to slow it down—to slow down the input that took me from innocence to chaos on a monthly basis. From a young age, my inner voice served as the loudest person in every room, screaming at me to be different, to look different, to act differently. Sensory overload would quickly turn a young, talented girl into a troubled teen who desperately needed to escape.

It seemed that feeling nothing was a better alternative than listening to the critical, judgmental girl yelling inside my head. From the time I was thirteen, my coping mechanism involved smoking marijuana, drinking, and taking prescription pain pills. The term *self-medicate* was an understatement: I was never sober. All my broken pieces were glued together by getting high and forgetting the worries and doubts that brewed inside of me. I didn't have to think or feel anything, my life was pleasantly clouded. I was accepted by my 'peers", the ones who were trying to forget, trying to become, trying to have fun, trying to not be alone.

I didn't have a care in the world when I dropped out of school in the ninth grade, saving myself from the anguish and torture of the high school hallways where being different felt out of reach, being myself seemed to hold me back, and being poor felt like a curse. Looking back, I realize that my school wasn't all that bad. Growing up in a military community was naturally diverse and atypical. My struggles were more internal, and I felt more lost than anything else.

I've never felt so empty, drained, and lost than when I was forced to spend countless hours inside a cement cage 'learning'. Being surrounded by so many people at once, everyone busily moving from class to class, talking, congregating, and creating noise made my head spin. Lockers slamming shut, people laughing, and voices over the intercom, even the squeaking of sneakers on the floor made me want to scream. Every noise seemed to be intentional and every bit of laughter seemed to be directed at me.

I skipped school often when I couldn't bear getting out of bed to leave the comfort of quiet isolation. There was nothing that scared me more than going to high school and there was no one that could force me to go. Rebellion became my defense mechanism and every disciplinary measure failed miserably. During hell week, every simple auditory disturbance drove me over the edge and pushed me into a full-on panic attack. Looking back, I realize why classrooms and hallways were excruciating for me during those times and why I avoided them at all costs.

When I did make it to class, I wasn't present; my energy was spent figuratively hiding from the chaos. I was the quiet introvert sitting in the back row observing the interactions between people, attempting to make sense of my extraverted surroundings. The teachers, busy with disruptive students, didn't even know my name most of the time. I would speak up when I was interested in a topic and blurted out an answer or two, but this was always done without my conscious consent. It was more like a reaction that hadn't been thought through. I turned in just enough work to not draw attention to myself and maintain a low profile.

This sudden shift would catch my mother off guard. Before high school I was a good kid with straight A's and numerous academic accomplishments. As a single mother, my grades were one thing she never had to worry about. From an incredibly young age I was driven and motivated to learn. When my older brother learned to read, I was the toddler who demanded his books so that I could learn too. With little effort I was top of my class and scored highly on academic tests.

Around age thirteen, when I started my period, my behavior took a turn for the worse, and no one would know why until decades later. My mother took me to psychologists and family doctors, trying to figure out what was wrong. I didn't have the manic episodes of bipolar and my symptoms weren't persistent. They told my mom time and time again that I was normal and healthy, I was simply a rebellious young lady. The stigma of being a teenage girl with an attitude problem defined who I was, eliminating the need for anyone to examine my behavior closer.

My PMDD would go undiagnosed for the next 20 years, causing a great deal of hardship in my life. I bounced around to different alternative schools and relatives, fighting my mother every step of the way. After two years of unrelenting bad behavior, we both felt a sense of relief when she stopped trying to force me to do anything. When I was fifteen, she gave up completely and I moved out of the family home and in with a group of older friends. She would let me go through my 'phase' in peace.

I found a part-time job working under the table at a dog grooming shop and earned just enough income to support my lifestyle. It was a peaceful time, just me and random furry friends to take care of. The animals didn't mind if I was having a bad day and if I needed to cry, that was ok too. They were there to listen to my rants without judgement as I talked to them about my newfound life. After work I was surrounded by great friends, neighborhood comedians, loud music, and plenty of drugs.

Responsibilities were minimal and we partied like poor rock stars every single day. I had my self-medicating routine down to a science, though at the time I had no idea that I was treating symptoms of PMDD. Life was great and the friendships I made would last a lifetime.

After a few incredible years, my time there would come to an abrupt halt as I refocused on responsibilities described in the next chapter of this book. My undiagnosed mental illness combined with a deep-rooted rebellion against uniformity and convention created conflict, but it also gave me great insight and depth, shaping the person I became along the way.

In my thirties I revisited drugs from a much different perspective. By this time, I'd traded in the drugs of my youth to become a responsible, high functioning alcoholic. The mechanism was different, but the reason was the same; I needed to escape my thoughts 25% of the time. The other 75% would be spent cleaning up the disasters I created during hell week, so I continued drinking afterwards too. My addiction to alcohol exacerbated my PMDD symptoms and I quickly took a turn for the worse.

At the end of 2019, when I started this book, I was diagnosed with PMDD after my suicidal ideation worsened. My doctor recommended that I track my mood on a calendar and bring the results to our next appointment. I presented my calendar to him, lined with red Xs for seven to eight days straight before my period started. The other days were marked with mixed results as I explained the challenges in my life, most of which originated during and were the result of hell week. My diagnosis became crystal clear and I was prescribed birth control pills to help control my symptoms. It helped a little, but my symptoms were still severe, and I was faced with the decision to start antidepressants. After twenty years of turmoil and a severe lack of scientific research I didn't trust that my doctor would get it right the first time around. I knew that I may have to try several different types and I wasn't convinced any of them would work. I didn't have time to wait three months to try one and see if it helped. My life was an urgent matter.

After turning down the pharmaceuticals (like I needed something else to become addicted to?) I began researching natural alternatives to help manage my PMDD symptoms. The lack of scientific research was discouraging. I found only a handful of scientific papers that were helpful. One paper published in 2017 by the National Institutes of Health[2] found that PMDD is linked to a sex-hormone sensitive gene complex, establishing a biological basis for the disorder. The monthly fluctuation in hormones is believed to cause a sensitivity resulting in altered brain chemicals and neurological pathways responsible for mood regulation and the feeling of well-being. After reading this, I began to have a glimmer of hope because understanding a problem is the first step towards resolution.

Although there is only anecdotal evidence of PMDD dating back to ancient times, one could assume that this gene mutation didn't just pop up a few years ago. Some women had undoubtedly suffered silently for far too long throughout history, and I refused to be the next one in a long line of misdiagnosed, misunderstood, and mistreated women who, before the onset of information technology, would have been ostracized and criticized, maybe even committed.

Even with the scientific breakthrough in 2017, treatment options are limited, and more research is needed. Many women, like myself, were fed up with the lack of knowledge and understanding. I didn't expect a cure, but I did need help to function at times.

After a quick Google search, I came across several online forums for PMDD sufferers. I carefully studied their first-hand accounts of treatments and self-reported results. This was a group of women I could trust; they described their symptoms and knew what worked. Some women reported success with antidepressants, while some opted for full hysterectomies to alleviate the suffering. Others, however, took matters into their own hands after being fed up with the medical community.

The forums were unique, diverse, anonymous accounts of women from various socioeconomic backgrounds, races, and age groups. Treatments were discussed but never debated, we all knew the pain that we already endured. This was no place for judgement. A few posts caught my eye; some women, desperate for relief, turned to microdosing psychedelics to alleviate their symptoms during hell week.

Psilocybin, the chemical found in "magic" mushrooms, was proving to be a valid alternative for sufferers who had exhausted other options or wanted something more natural. Research[3] on hallucinogenic treatment for mental health disorders started back in the 1950's, but the war on drugs quickly disabled the efforts when psilocybin and LSD were classified as schedule one drugs. Now, research was slowly gaining traction again, and with the use of the Internet, underground communities made their way to online platforms like Reddit to discuss their own strategies. Microdosing seemed promising; I could include it into my routine with little disruption to my life. A small fraction of a normal dose, taken every three days was reportedly producing great results for sufferers of a wide range of mental health disorders.

People from all walks of life were embracing not only the relief of depression and anxiety but also the increase in general self-development, creativity, and focus. There is no evidence of addiction or withdrawal symptoms when you stop taking it. Slight nausea can occur after ingestion and of course if you take too much you may hallucinate, or 'trip'. A microdose doesn't contain enough of the drug to cause hallucinations, which was even more appealing to me. I didn't really have time on my calendar for full-on psychedelic trips.

For some reason, hallucinogens didn't make an appearance during my teenage years, though I believe they would have helped me tremendously. Due to my lack of experience with the drug, I was a bit scared of the widely publicized 'bad trip' that some people encountered.

That was, until the day I accidentally macrodosed. As many researchers point out, psilocybin is still an illegal substance and we don't have a good mechanism to control dosage outside of the lab. Taking too much can lead to a hallucinogenic trip and taking too little won't produce the desired effects.

I fully understood the risks associated with my decision, but they were a drop in the bucket to me compared to antidepressants or doing nothing to manage my symptoms. I was familiar with acquiring my own drugs from trusted sources and I was surprised at the wealth of knowledge you can find online. From the organic growing process to acquiring supplies and grow kits, it's all there.

I was also surprised to find that Denver, Colorado became the first place in the US to effectively decriminalize the use of magic mushrooms[4] in adults over the age of twenty-one, with California and Oregon pushing similar legislation. The growing body of research was supporting these initiatives and educating the masses on not only possible medicinal applications for mental health but also the lack of evidence for addiction and abuse.

Adding it to my routine of meditation, visualization techniques, and yoga, microdosing became an integral part of my self-care routine. During my 25% I would up the dose slightly to manage my mood and alleviate symptoms.

One Sunday afternoon, after receiving a fresh batch and knowing that hell week was approaching, I doubled my normal dose. My microdose routine included one spoonful of a honey and mushroom mixture every three days; a double dose would normally heighten my mood just enough to prevent PMDD symptoms from taking over my life but not enough to cause hallucinations. Anyone that has eaten psilocybin mushrooms before knows how terrible the taste is and the honey helped.

Two spoonful's later and I was lying in bed hovering over myself, in a deeply relaxed state. The mushrooms were far more concentrated than the previous batch and I found myself in the middle of a vivid visualization. It was as if the floodgates of my thoughts opened and were finally able to mix between compartments, creating connections and enabling me to think in a way that I hadn't been able to before.

An incredibly happy woman appeared at the top of a flight of stairs. She was radiant, glowing with a smile from ear to ear. She was sexy and unapologetic, gliding gracefully down each step with a confident catwalk that could only be found on the runway. The world around me stopped spinning as each word that she spoke flowed freely from her soul with absolute authenticity. She was the center of attention as all my senses tuned into her greatness.

I could touch her perfume, feel the sounds that her heels made on the steps, and taste the oxygen that she breathed in. Her glow illuminated the room and shined down on my skin like a warm, summer day. She wore a white lab coat with black framed glasses, and a tight black dress with high heels. Her figure was perfect, and the dress hugged her body as if every inch of the fabric was carefully constructed just for her. Her long dark hair fell to the small of her back with a few perfect curls bouncing at the ends. Her hazel eyes were bright with a mesmerizing sparkle and her skin was flawless.

Each of these features were amplified in my senses as were colors and sounds; she was larger than life though not physically, and it was like I was watching a movie in vivid Technicolor.

Femininity poured into every crevice of the room creating a peaceful space filled with forgiveness and compassion. I felt an amazing, indescribable sense of calm rush over my body. It was as if I was looking directly into the person I wanted to become. The woman that was buried under layers of my poorly written self-image.

The staircase was dark and romantic, and the air was heavy, surrounding me like a warm blanket. As the woman approached the end of the staircase, I followed her to a space in the corner of a dark basement, though I never actually left my bed. The room was bright white and sterile resembling a homemade lab of sorts. I melted into a small bed in the corner and pulled the silk sheets over my skin. The woman sat down next to me, holding my hand while she thoroughly examined my thoughts.

She was a best friend, mother, sister, and doctor, fully dedicated to caring for me. She directed my attention to a set of server racks a few feet over, pointing out the bright blue glow of lights. Endless bundles of unorganized cables created a complex grid and I struggled to trace them with my eyes. This tiny, chaotic, data center ran my program; I knew that this was where my thoughts were being processed. This was where data was being exchanged with the outside world. Input and output ran like some fast-motion system of roadways, orderly and chaotic at the same time. Information was filtered and transformed through the programs I unknowingly created throughout my lifetime, and I could now see them with clarity, neatly compartmentalized.

The woman was not only my caretaker and nurturer, she was my programmer. She was there to help me rewrite the shitty, highly flawed programs I created for myself over the years. When she opened her laptop, the keystrokes rang out like music to my ears as she began to program love songs into my soul. Her aura filled the basement from wall to wall and transformed the air into mesmerizing energy. She was the master of her craft, intently

13

focused on each line of code with surgical precision. Locked into a flow state, I felt the goosebumps on her skin as she poured her heart and soul into her life's work. It was a feeling I would soon experience for myself as I wrote this book.

I fell deeply in love with her and the process that was unfolding in front of me. The version of life that I was living could change, and with work it could evolve into whatever I wanted it to be. Just like rewriting the program. Just like updating the software. Just like inventing a new computer game where I was the superhero, the protagonist, the star of my own life.

As the psilocybin began to wear off, that euphoric experience would haunt me in the most beautiful way, shaping the reflections lined out in this book.

The visualization of the woman was a vivid, life altering encounter. On the surface, it could be described as a hallucination, but there were layers that I wanted to better understand. My experience, or epiphany wasn't like a traditional trip, and the dose wasn't high enough to elicit hallucinations of that magnitude. The only explanation I have for the experience is heightened creativity and focus, it was art, my own version of a masterpiece. It was deep meditation on steroids mixed harmoniously with the visualization techniques that I had been practicing. It was Carlos Castaneda meets Maharishi Mahesh Yogi.

The analyst in me desperately wanted to know how it worked. I went back to review research and learn more about the effects of psilocybin on the brain. A double-blind study performed by Johns Hopkins found that a single high dose of psilocybin showed an improvement in clinically depressed mood for 80% of study subjects suffering from cancer-related anxiety and depression.[1] The research went on to demonstrate that of the subjects who improved, the majority of them experienced sustained, positive effects on their mood, lasting up to six months after the single dose.

Dr. Roland Griffiths, Professor in the Departments of Psychiatry and Neurosciences at the Johns Hopkins University School of Medicine and a leading psychopharmacologist, pointed out in his TedMed talk[5], *The science of psilocybin and its use to relieve suffering*, that these results, although preliminary, "are unprecedented in the field of psychiatry". Through my own personal experience, I wholeheartedly agreed with the findings.

While PMDD is not well understood, scientists speculate that during hell week, the week before the menstrual cycle, there is a disruption in normal serotonin processes that regulate mood. Psilocybin binds with serotonin

14

receptors creating a sense of euphoria and well-being; microdosing was a brilliant remedy for my 25% of hell. What I didn't realize was the profound impact that psilocybin would have on my 75%.

Behind the scenes in my brain, the substance was reducing the activity of what is called the default mode network, or the DMN for short. The DMN helps us complete tasks and runs our autopilot to create efficiencies in our day to day life. This network carries information across regions of the brain that are responsible for our self-image, making tiny decisions on our behalf along the way. It's like reading this:

Cna oyu rdea htis stneence?

You've seen these words before, and your brain quickly deciphers the letters to match the most likely words it has recorded in your memory. This is highly efficient. You don't have to consciously figure out what the words are supposed to be. The DMN has made the decision to correct automatically.

For people with a positive self-image, this network operates in their favor as they move through life on autopilot, locked onto dream destinations. For someone like me, however, it would work against me, making poor decisions until I put in the work to reprogram it.

My experience on mushrooms started to make sense as I learned that psilocybin hijacks the blood flow from the DMN essentially removing the handcuffs of my predetermined self-image, the image that PMDD helped me create throughout my life. This so-called 'ego dissolution'[6] acted like a reset button, removing the garbage that had been stored over the years. There was no subjective judgement, all of which was an illusion.

Blood flow was redirected to other areas of the brain, enabling unconstrained cognition and increased creativity. During the process, my brain made new connections to alternate regions, strengthening information pathways that weren't well traveled before.[7] My brain built new highways, also known as neuroplasticity, and the traffic started flowing freely. The visualization of the woman in the basement was simply a creative expression of my technical knowledge as a systems analyst mixed with a deep rooted desire to remove every constraint in my life, especially those that I unknowingly created for myself.

Over the next few months, the visualization would shape the methodology I used to reprogram my life, finally learning how to live a life worth living, even during my 25%. The person I was before my experience with mushrooms

15

began to change and form a more meaningful existence. My alcoholism went from several drinks a day to an occasional beer on the weekend. My self-care routine became a priority, and I began respecting myself as much as I respected the woman in the basement.

Through the process, many of the things that used to trouble me fell out of focus while my life's work took center stage. I felt her goosebumps while writing, the sound of my keystrokes rang out like a musical masterpiece, her smile became my own, her mesmerizing energy filled my bedroom and the thoughts of suicide faded away like a distant sunset.

DELETE EXPECTATIONS

"For me, a life without expectation results in a life with inspiration."

(Alanis Morissette)

To the outside world, my life seemed oddly put together. I did a great job hiding my feelings, especially from myself when I doused them with mind altering substances. In reality I was quietly walking up a flight of stairs, playing with a yo-yo, floating through the ups and downs like a teary-eyed champion. I discovered at an early age that life didn't come with instructions, and just like everyone else, I'd have to figure it out along the way.

The hardest lessons would be the most meaningful and every challenge would push me closer to becoming the disastrous woman I was meant to be. Expectations of the world and of myself would result in great joy and disappointment as I unknowingly navigated my rollercoaster of emotions. Inspiration would appear at my lowest points, as if it were ultimately designed to disrupt the chaos of someone falling too deep into their own despair.

At seventeen my life changed suddenly when I found out I was pregnant with my daughter. In obvious self-reflection, I was not prepared to raise a child; I could barely care for myself. I had no desire to have children, especially not at seventeen. My boyfriend at the time, expressed a completely different sentiment towards the situation. He had won a battle with cancer several years before, but the doctor told him that his chances of having children were slim. While the surprise was difficult for me to process, to him, he was experiencing a modern-day miracle and couldn't have been more excited.

He came from a middle-class family and his relationship with his parents was strong, unlike my troubled encounters with my mother. He had a support system to fall back on, something I knew little about. He was elated while I was devastated. The news made my head spin as I searched for the right words and actions to deal with the situation. The decision was complex, and I don't subscribe well to other people's guidance about my personal choices. My values system at seventeen was as unwavering as they are today at thirty-three, and I still stand behind the decision I made. I couldn't rob this man of what may have been his only chance at having a child. With mixed feelings, I decided to have a baby.

I'll never forget the day when I returned home to tell my mother. She told me to leave as the screen door slammed in my face. Her response caught me off guard, not because she didn't approve, but because of her anger. She was infuriated in a way that I'd never seen her before. Raw emotion spewed from every bone in her body, her frustration and disappointment projected at me until I sunk into a much smaller person. Her expectations of the person I should have become were shattered in real time. She was right in a way. My 'phase' would last a lifetime. But she was wrong to believe that my phase wouldn't ultimately serve me well and offer me something on many levels I could have never otherwise known and experienced.

In her mind, the bright toddler with bouncy curls would not grow up to be a doctor or a lawyer, she likely wouldn't even finish high school. She would be destined for a life on welfare and food stamps, never having the opportunity to fulfill her potential. She would struggle immensely, just like her mother did. She would continue the cycle and become the third generation of women without a college education or meaningful career.

Her expectations of the next chapters in my life couldn't have been more wrong. Her feelings towards me were nothing more than a reflection of her own misery, shame, and disappointment. She was trapped in a life where her greatness had fallen out of reach. She was the artist who stopped creating, derailed from her lifelong passion so she could make a living and raise her children. Always putting herself last, her greatness had been quickly and efficiently muted. Her gifts were bottled up so tightly that the flame in her soul barely flickered, suffocated by the daily responsibilities she had inadvertently imposed on herself. Her head had been swiftly pulled out of the clouds.

At the time, I felt abandoned, alone and disillusioned in a world I knew little about, carrying the makings of a woman that I didn't know how to put together. The thought of not having a parent to help me along the journey was frightening, but looking back, the lessons were carefully weaved in. I quickly gave up any hope of help from my family. My mother was out of the equation; she wouldn't even speak to me. With a baby on the way, the next few months were an incredible race to get my shit together. I realized during that time that intellect was my ally, it was all I had up my sleeve. I may have skipped most of my classes, but I was born with intelligence and I could use it to my advantage.

I showed up to GED classes in the evening and joined a mixed bag of people. With an eighth-grade education, I didn't expect to do well. To my surprise, I had only been to two classes before the teacher told me to go ahead and take the test without finishing the rest of the course. I passed on my first attempt and beamed with hope as I refocused on getting a driver's license. Saving money to pay off court fines I had racked up for truancy, I was finally eligible for a license. My aunt and uncle threw me a surprise baby shower and delivered an old Mazda for me to drive. Their compassion and generosity left a mark on my soul, a piece of their greatness spilling over for me to enjoy. They paid $2000 for it and it ran like new, a gift that meant the absolute world to me, someone with only months to get her life together.

My expectations of what I could achieve in a matter of months were exceeded and I began to feel proud of my small accomplishments. Undoubtedly, pregnancy protected me from my own negative thoughts, allowing positivity to creep in for more than a few weeks at a time. With a GED, a driver's license, and a car, I found a job working at a grocery store with my boyfriend, earning a little more money than at the dog groomers. In a matter of six months my life was coming together. My boyfriend's family was busy picking out baby clothes, car seats and strollers. His mother helped me through my pregnancy, explaining Braxton Hicks contractions[8] and making sure I was eating well. We moved into a one-bedroom apartment and I started to feel at ease with my new life.

When my daughter finally came, I remember not sleeping for more than two hours at a time, not because she woke me up but because maternal instincts would not allow me to sleep. Next to my bed in a bassinet, I woke up to check that she was still there, still breathing, not crying, not hungry, not cold. For an inexperienced mom, I exceeded my own expectations. With my daughter in my arms, I wondered how a mother could leave their child in such a vulnerable situation, enduring the hardships of life on her own. I realize now that pulling myself up and finding my own way was the exact experience my life required.

A few short months later, sitting at the break-room table at work, I put my head down just for a moment to close my eyes. Tears began to swell up after I realized how tired I was. Picking up a second job at another grocery store was necessary to keep the bills paid. I enrolled in community college with the hope of breaking the cycle of poverty I was so well acquainted with. Working two jobs and taking online classes was almost impossible as a young mother. Add in a broken relationship with my mom and now my boyfriend, life got hard. Just because he might not have been able to have children didn't mean he was ready to be a father. Sleepless nights and the weight of the world are too heavy for some to bear.

My mood swings would start to creep up again as the fluctuations of hormones resumed in my body, and our arguments worsened. Relationships have never been my strong suit; growing up with a single mother I never got the memo that men were a relevant part of life. We fought about everything, from money to who was getting up with the baby to doing dishes after a long day at work. He didn't help even when he was there, so essentially, I was a single mother from day one. I was glad when he left, at least I wouldn't be expected to cook and clean up after him too.

Although encouraged to continue a relationship with his daughter, he would barely come around to help until years later, after he finally found his way in life. His greatness was stifled, stuck in a cycle of not knowing what to do, not knowing how to handle the pressure, not knowing that I was unwell when I reminded him of his shortcomings. His expectations of fatherhood were incredibly incorrect, forcing him into avoidance and denial for years. He would come into his role much later, just in time to care for her when I no longer could.

I fell in love with my daughter despite the hard times and challenges that surrounded her entrance into the world. When I wasn't at work, she played in my lap while I typed papers for online college. I was busy, but I handled every single responsibility and I was working hard to improve our lives. I remember the day when I was told that I made too much money for food stamps; I was making progress. Being just over the poverty line was something I was proud of. My expectations for life—at least as far as my limited world view was concerned at the time—were exceeded.

My success seed had now been planted, and as I kept climbing, my unlimited expectations were consistently met with a potential within myself that I had not so far been exposed to. And the more I achieved, the more successes I had and the more I continued to climb.

Although I was moving in the right direction, at this point I was running on fumes and gifted energy drinks from friends at the grocery store. The long days at work were excruciating and I only earned just enough to cover the bills. PMDD mood swings would continue to inspire me to change as I fell into deep depressions that included times of critical self-reflection. Hell week was a revolving reminder of what I believed to be my failures as a parent. I knew I could do better. At least that's what the person who lived through hell week told me. She believed that I could never do enough to bring myself up, that what I was doing was just not enough and never would be.

Regardless of the progress that I made, my own expectations—the expectations that I set during my 25%—were left unmet. Every time I built myself up, PMDD would come back just to knock me down and remind me that I was a little tiny nobody. One step forward, two steps back.

Despair, however, became my motivator. Even during my darkest hours, there was a tiny flame, something sparking in the shadows of that despair that kept reaching for me, like a light flickering in the fog, a beacon that kept my compass aiming in the right direction so I could find my way home. Buried in that fog, I started planning for a better life. I realized that I couldn't work two jobs forever and living just over the poverty line wasn't much to brag about. I didn't realize that this in itself was an accomplishment to be proud of. I just didn't see it back then. I didn't have sick days and taking a vacation to regroup and rejuvenate was completely out of the question. Growing up surrounded by a large Army community, the military was the major source of income in the area. Soldiers had nicer cars, paid college tuition, steady paychecks, benefits, and retirement plans. We had none of the above.

Desperate to escape my hell and build a better life for me and my daughter, I signed a three-year contract with the US Army. Looking around at my friends, I realized that if I wanted something different, I'd have to do something different. My desires and ambitions were met with massive action. It was 2008, the world was in a global financial crisis, and seven years had passed since the terrorist attacks of 9/11. The War on Terror was in full swing and I knew that I would likely deploy to the Middle East. Intimately familiar with the benefits of the military, war was a calculated risk that I was willing to take.

I kissed my daughter goodbye and hopped on a bus to basic training as I thanked both of her grandmothers and her aunt for helping while I was gone. Although I didn't have much luck with her father at the time, his mother and sister always rose to the occasion to help, and my mother soon realized the blessings of having her first grandchild. I knew she was in great hands with a village that loved her.

Reverting to the introverted girl in the back row, I kept my head down and held myself together at all costs, ensuring that the drill sergeants didn't know my name. Skipping sports growing up didn't help and I felt the burn of every single muscle in my body until they all went numb. The sound of my M16 would ring in my ears as the drill sergeants yelled at us from a distance. Knowing that we would likely deploy to combat immediately after training, we spent plenty of time at the weapons range honing our skills. Ruck marches were especially terrible as I discovered that my feet were the weakest link. Quarter sized blisters would appear after the first few miles forcing me to the back of our formation, tears stinging my hazel eyes, I hoped no one would notice.

In September 2010 I kissed my daughter goodbye once again and boarded a C130 aircraft with my equipment. Ready to touchdown in a combat zone, I wasn't convinced that I would return. Like the feeling of opening a hot oven, the blast of heat that surrounded my body when I first stepped off the plane in Iraq is one that I'll never forget. The brightness of the sun and the dust that covered my skin, the adrenaline of not knowing what to expect despite all of the training—all of that was alien, like something out of a movie, a science fiction movie. My M4 semi-automatic weapon stayed by my side, every second of every day for the next year.

Stationed in Mosul, the base had been around for several years and the makeshift living conditions weren't so bad. There was a laundry service, and the dining facility, lovingly called the DFAC, served three meals a day. I didn't have to worry about cooking or cleaning up the kitchen afterwards. The food was surprisingly good, and I had decent internet service. Anxiety would fade away with time, realizing that I was surrounded by thousands of trained killers with loaded weapons ready to die for the cause.

Fortunately, Mosul was quiet at the time and didn't have a lot of enemy movement. My job kept me stationary setting up critical communications and surveillance platforms to keep an eye on our surroundings. We were the silent nerds in the back, a necessary component of war.

The military taught me a great deal about life. I made friendships that have lasted a lifetime and gained discipline skills that still serve me well. Most of all, I learned how to take calculated risks. When I got out of the service, I was well suited for the next round of major improvements in my life, or so I thought at the time.

Ignoring my mood swings, I kept pushing despite the ups and downs, and by age thirty I had achieved everything on my list and then some. I now had a master's degree paid for by the military and a great job at a startup tech company. I was safe from the war and lived in a free country; I could be and do whatever I wanted. I lived in a beautiful home and drove a nicer car. I was married to a successful man I met in the Army, and my daughter now had a little brother. I defied all statistics and by all measures I had made something of myself.

From the outside looking in, life was perfect. My relationship with my mother improved and we hosted family gatherings together for the holidays. Her expectations of my life were exceeded, and she now bragged about my accomplishments to her friends. From the girl that dropped out of school to the appearance of a strong successful woman, my life went in a straight line towards a destination that I knew nothing about.

My success story soon started to fade away, however, transforming into a nightmarish plot as I once again began to spin out of control. After years of hard work, I expected to be happy with myself, I expected to be proud of my accomplishments. I did everything right; I finished college, I worked hard, I made more money, I worked out, I ate well, but I was still mostly miserable. I was ok at times, but my 25% would drag me down to the pits of hell where I found myself critiquing every tiny detail of my life—again.

After only a few years of marriage, we signed divorce paperwork, finally putting an end to the hallways of hell in our home. I traded in my job at the startup for a "better" job in 'Corporate America', demanding a higher salary, ironically just to invite more misery and struggle into my life. Long commutes were spent gazing out the window at the beautiful sunset, an orange and pink painted sky. Three hours alone every day gave me plenty of time to think about which bridge I should drive my car over to end my cycle of suffering.

Nothing was ever good enough for the judgmental voices that rang out in my head. The girl who fought like hell against the statistics was trapped in a cycle of negative self-talk, putting her back in her place as soon as she started making progress. Every month led me to a new action, desperate to find happiness and peace. Break up, make up, new shoes, new coping mechanism, new class, new certification, new plan, new job, new self-help book, new sheets, new restaurant; nothing ever satisfied my unrelenting urge to improve.

Self-help books reminded me that I had control over my life, I needed to take more risks and take massive action. I needed to do something I had never done before to escape my unhappiness. Feeling trapped, I had to choose between having more time for myself and my kids or more money in my bank account. Any subsequent promotions in my field would send me up the corporate ladder, trading my precious time for more stress and more money. My unlimited potential was capped within a framework of corporate politics and hierarchy.

My chest tightened and the air grew heavy as I thought about the rest of my life being defined by the structure of corporatism. Days filled with needless meetings, negotiating with management, and having forced relationships with people I didn't really care about. Sleepless nights were filled with anxiety and I felt endless pressure to do more and be better. Long commutes and even longer days were spent spinning my wheels and honing knowledge that would go unused and unapplied. The thought of doing this for the rest of my life was too much to bear. Discontentment filled my soul and negativity was baked into every word I spoke. I had finally hit my brick wall. I quit my corporate job with only three months' worth of expenses saved. My only plan was to buy myself time to think and breathe.

Reflecting on the shit show that was my life, I started to wonder why I allowed runaway expectations to run my life, why I kept choosing things that no longer served me. I never thought that my expectations were too high, just extremely misguided. Torturing myself for years through internal dialogue, I never took the time to sort through it and just feel it. I just expected to work hard and be happy as a result.

As it turned out, hitting my brick wall was the absolute best thing that could have happened. It forced me to be objective about my own expectations of the world. Expectation is inherently fuzzy and as hard as you try, you'll never know all the variables. Things far outside of your control will throw you off course and leave you drained while you try to pick up the pieces of your life.

Who the hell was I to predict the beautiful roadblocks that would throw me off course? Expectations are limiting as well as limited; they're limited by what you can create from your experience, and limiting because you can only see those designs you create, those things you believe can be true for you. Your happiness, therefore, is a product of your subjective response to your own world view and opinion about yourself, that very opinion that is both limited and limiting. Your self-image—what you believe about yourself—will be gauged accordingly.

Not hitting your wall, your peak of emotion, your breaking point early enough is the most tragic thing that can happen to one's life. Eventually the day will come when it's too late, the day that you'll wonder if your life was meaningful enough, if you touched enough people with your incredible gifts, if you lived up to your absolute potential. PMDD may have caused some hardships, but I accept it as my own, as if it's my remarkably talented wild child always causing trouble.

The deep self-reflection and life review that I experienced every month can only be compared to someone closer to death than life. Someone who is forced to analyze their time here on earth and determine if their life is still worth living.

I've been fortunate enough to receive a gift: enlightening, inspiring despair every month. Through years of intensive training, I've learned powerful resilience that's only available to a select group of women.[9] Silently behind the scenes, we learn the powers of the mind and remarkable absolute truths about how our own thoughts can sabotage everything if we let them wander too far outside of our control.

The switch that we experience demonstrates how good and evil can be brought into plain view, illuminating the depths of humanity in ways that most people will never experience on a recurring basis, if at all. We are the fortunate few who experience extreme hopelessness just long enough to truly understand it, but not long enough to stop us from helping others out of it. We can meet people where they are, we see the light that shines through the darkness in humanity, and we help people up, knowing that their despair doesn't define them. We've learned how to pull ourselves back and deter the brainwashing techniques that our mind uses on us. We are intimately familiar with the mind's methods of self-harm and negative self-imagery.

All this time I thought that I was a failure, but in reality, I was training for something much larger than myself. There's no way I could have expected my disorder. There's no way I could have expected the development of my unique outlook on something that appeared so terrible on its surface. After my diagnosis, I removed all expectations and found a way to just be, to accept all things as they are, to listen to the beautiful frequency of my own song, dimmed over the years by social pressures and crippling expectations.

The longer we hold onto the expectations we've set for our lives, our gifts, and our talents, the longer we remain closed to understanding the wisdom pouring out of our souls and receiving the blessings the universe has for us, the only things that actually matter. It's not up to you to define or expect your own greatness, your only responsibility is to nurture it and allow enough space for it to thrive.

REVERSE ENGINEER

"If you wish to find yourself, you must first admit you are lost."

(Brian Rathbone, *Call of the Herald*)

T iny moments from our past can have such significant impact on the person we become, but we fail to notice those moments until we stop and look between the lines. The first version of who you were was not created by you, but rather a mixture of DNA, experiences, and upbringing that were far outside of your control. Until we slow down and intimately reflect, we don't stand a chance at change and we will continue to limp through life being a simple product of our environment. Human creation is too powerful to be swayed easily once the foundation is set.

Ironically, as difficult as it might seem on the surface to make corrections that can change the course of life by changing mindset or the way your mind thinks, it's really just a matter of one simple act, but that act must be enforced consistently, just like any habit, in order for it to take hold. For most, consistency is within reach. For PMDD sufferers, however, we must form the habit of loving ourselves despite it. We are the tribe of the consistently inconsistent.

Powerful change can only occur with the right tools and proper mindset. We must first come to terms with the fact that we didn't create our initial selves, it was built for us, the good the bad and the ugly. Our parents, our siblings, and our teachers all played a role in building our tiny child world, and this was all we knew. The idea of being unwell or requiring space at times was never embraced or understood; we were supposed to be like everyone else, we were supposed to be normal. That was the model from which we subconsciously drew our experience and around which we built our initial world. In order to absolve ourselves of this we must first understand and accept it as truth. Only then will it be freeing and allow us the space to open up to actual change. After we accept where we are and how we got there, we have a life changing choice to make. We can continue through life with what's been given to us or we can reverse engineer and rebuild from the ground up, keeping the good experiences and relinquishing the bad.

My mind, which was terrorized by a terrible disorder, was struggling to find homeostasis. In that struggle, the pendulum swung in the opposite direction and forced me into a space of wholeness and peace within myself and the world around me.

PMDD provided me with a unique perspective into a complex system that can work for or against us. If the disorder taught me anything at all it is the hard and fast lesson that we can change rapidly for better or for worse in a matter of days. Just as fast as we can downward spiral into despair, we can redirect our energy towards something much more positive, more meaningful and edifying.

Enduring a healing journey is bittersweet because finding the light requires tracing the footsteps of your darkest days. If the process is 100% pleasant, you're probably doing it wrong and creating shortcuts that dilute the remedy. Dedication is required, you must confront your demons face to face and never back down despite how uncomfortable it is to look directly into your failures or shortcomings. Humans are messy, a patchwork of pieced together experiences, social conventions, and individual egos. You are messy too, there's no escaping that and there's nowhere to hide.

The fire that burns inside of each of us can light up the room that we walk into or burn down a village. There comes a time when we are forced to set an intention for which one we want. The idea that we have free will is only valid if we are intentional about our thoughts and actions. Otherwise we're just wandering through life like drones, living at the mercy of our unintentional versions. In other words, the world is going to act upon you whether you're aware of it or not, so wouldn't it be better to bend the world to your will rather than having it bend you? Miserable outcomes don't have to be repeated throughout life, but without accepting who you are, and without putting in the work, you'd be a fool to expect anything more than what you already have.

Quitting my job gave me the mental space I needed to survive but it came with great financial risk. In my twenties, I always planned on making more money rather than paying attention to what I did with what I had. Hell week led me to department stores - more dresses and shoes to lift my spirits and make me feel whole again.

In my early thirties my income went from $50,000 to $100,000 a year, doubling in less than three years. My decision to walk away from my career wasn't easy, but I'd do it again in a heartbeat, not because the next chapter was going to be pleasant but because it was necessary. Realizing that my money wouldn't last long, I had to come up with a plan for my next move. Taking inventory of my assets, I had closets filled with stuff I never wore in a house that didn't feel like home. It was summer of 2019 and the housing market was booming. Looking around at the hallways of hell, I decided to give it up and sell my house.

This was the first point in my life when I stopped planning what came next. I wasn't sure where I'd go or what I'd do but getting rid of my mortgage payment and refilling my bank account would buy me time to think. The next few weeks were spent painting, watering dead grass and getting to know a stranger who had crossed my path. A random conversation with a friend led to my confession of wanting to disappear for a night, just to get out of the house and be an adult again in the middle of my chaos.

A week later and I was at a hole in the wall bar with an interesting, dark haired friend of a friend having drinks. I was caught off guard at first by how attractive he was, only to be even more surprised by his conversation and even-tempered mood. After my divorce, I stayed secluded and guarded, with no intention of having a serious relationship for quite some time. As the months went on, I felt the loneliness creep in. Human nature knocking on my door telling me I had needs too.

My problems faded away while I tuned into the present moments of our endless conservations. The two of us lingered for hours under the Austin moonlight, chatting on the patio until the bar closed. We were pleasantly authentic and natural, never overbearing, or awkward. He was a great guy from a good family, calm and logical but he still knew how to have fun. We couldn't have been more different; he had never been married, had no children, came from a well-off family, and invested his money wisely over the years. I remember thinking I could learn from him, though at the time I had no idea about the powerful lessons he would later bring into my life.

He was incredibly whole, it seemed as though he wasn't missing any pieces, he was grounded in who he was as a person, and his presence was refreshing. The time we spent together was nothing short of amazing, I called him the island, my vacation away from life. I was a different person when I was with him, I didn't talk about my worries or concerns, and I was present in every peaceful moment of happiness and desire. We kept things consistent yet at a reasonable distance, sharing just enough of ourselves to spend time on our island in peaceful bliss.

Despite our brilliant rendezvous, my mainland was in silent shambles and money was only one of my many concerns. Keeping my island at a distance was crucial as I navigated my newfound relationship with my ex-husband. We were learning how to agree to disagree and ensuring we worked together to raise our children in harmony. Surrounded by the military my entire life, unfortunately, PMDD wasn't the only mental illness that I became intimately familiar with.

Many soldiers' experiences in combat were far different than my own. Being sent to battle during the onset of the war, soldiers endured a completely different battleground. By the time I met my ex-husband, he already had the mental battle scars that started to bubble up over time. After a rough childhood, he signed up to serve, deploying to Iraq for the first time before he was old enough to drink. The body count was much higher, the enemy was in full swing, and the living arrangements were subpar, far below what I experienced in Mosul.

Although our divorce was mutual, he wasn't adjusting well to life on his own. I started to notice his depression and anxious behavior worsen when he dropped off our son every other week. Struggling to find his own way, he began floating the idea of moving home to Indiana, suggesting that being closer to friends and family would help. For many, this situation may have led to arguments or questions on custody arrangements. For us, it was a moment of agreement, a moment of understanding and compassion, a moment of meeting each other where we were and not expecting an ounce more.

Every day, seventeen veterans die from suicide.[10] The toll of war perpetuates for years afterwards, holding veterans hostage in their own minds. Ordinary people trying to earn a living, pay for college and make something of themselves became prisoners of their memories. I saw exactly where he was, and although I was no longer his wife, I couldn't turn my back on a fellow veteran in need. Knowing that he wouldn't leave without his son, we came up with a plan—we'd all move. In a matter of weeks, I had a full offer on my house, freeing up $30,000 in cash. My son and his dad were on their way to

Indiana and I was busy explaining my plans to friends, family, and my new boyfriend.

Although many didn't understand, they all pitched in to help. My boyfriend helped me pack the few things that I decided to bring with me in my Toyota leaving enough room for my dog in the front seat. We kissed each other goodbye and I left my home state of Texas to move to the Midwest.

Working through the scenario gracefully, we continued to date from a distance, planning trips to meet up in nearby Chicago to continue to get to know each other. Preserving my way of life became a priority even as my money began to dwindle. I knew that I couldn't keep this up forever, money went out every month but there was nothing coming in to replace it. I was okay for a while, but I'd have to find a way to make income.

Refusing to go back to work full time, I researched different ways to earn money and stumbled upon the website, bizbuysell.com, a platform for buying and selling small businesses. I wondered if I could purchase one with the remaining cash I had on hand. If I could just make enough money to maintain my lifestyle I could continue to hide from the world until I figured out what I wanted to do long term.

Scrolling through the site, I found a small party rental company performing a quick sale; the list price was $9,500, just in my budget. Jumping on the opportunity, I fired off an email to get more information. I researched the company's reputation, read online reviews, and studied the financials provided by the seller. In two short weeks I owned a business and my tiny apartment was filled with party rental equipment. There was $7,000 in pre-booked business so there was no time to spare in getting set up.

As usual, I moved with urgency and massive action. Marketing and sales were enhanced by a fresh website and I expanded advertising to capture new markets. Two employees quickly grew to five and booked revenue for the year went from $7,000 to $20,000. My plan was to run the business from the sidelines, doing the work behind the scenes. This was a lifestyle business and my ideal lifestyle was hiding from people. With a bit of money to fall back on I started making investments back into the business. I bought new equipment and new software and offered paid training for my employees. The money came in and went right back out. The overhead grew with the revenue and I even started to add expenses to a business credit card.

My boyfriend was incredibly encouraging and offered his guidance and input whenever I asked for it. Always an amazing listener, he was a sounding board for my ideas and helped me formulate plans. My fiery passion was met with his even-tempered mood, we were a balanced force of energy and we both knew it. We grew closer with distance and began to miss the days of being on the island together. Drawn to each other, we started making plans for the next step.

After some gentle persuasion and a few trips to remind him what he was missing, he decided to move to Indiana to continue our love affair in person. He offered to help me with my business, work events with me and help improve operations. As an independent investor, he was flexible with time, location, and money, a lifestyle I knew nothing about. I was eager to learn from him and excited about being on the island full time. I felt like my life was moving in the right direction and things were coming together.

He would keep his house in Texas to use when he came back, which would turn out to be much sooner than he realized. October is beautiful in Texas, finally cooling down after a long grueling summer, and it was the perfect time to load the small moving truck and do a road trip across the country. The long drive provided us an opportunity to talk about our plans, the business, and our new life together. We talked, we laughed, and we enjoyed each other's company for a seemingly short, eight-hour trip before stopping for the night. I remember feeling very tired but happy and hopeful for our next chapter.

The next day we would wake up and continue our drive, stopping for a quick bite to eat and extra-large cups of coffee. Pulling into the driveway late at night we unloaded just enough to get settled and get some sleep.

The next morning, I woke up early to a cup of coffee that he made for me, a gesture that never went unnoticed throughout our relationship. We went straight to work unloading the truck, knowing we had a lot to do to get settled in. Starting to feel a bit off, I felt my energy begin to drain before I even got started. Looking around, there was so much to do and a limited time to do it. Feeling anxious, rushes of fight or flight hormones began flowing through my body and my breathing became heavier.

I vividly remember every box I helped carry into the house, struggling to hold a conversation with him as I tried to focus intently on every step I made. My phone wouldn't stop ringing and the text alerts made me cringe until I finally silenced it, hiding from the noise. Every step from the truck to the house was a minute to reflect and try to make sense of what was going on in my head. The all-to-familiar feeling of intense fear bubbled up and my stress level skyrocketed as I looked at a living room full of boxes.

I didn't know where anything would go, I was confused, disoriented, and overwhelmed. I got quiet and hid my pop-up emotions well, but they wouldn't let me go, I couldn't snap out of it, the PMDD trance was taking over and I began thinking about every reason why my relationship was going to fail. I began frantically worrying about how my kids were going to adapt to him, despite our numerous discussions prior to the move. I felt like I was making a terrible mistake. I asked myself if I was a bad parent for running away with my boyfriend the last few days to help him move.

My gut reaction was that this man wasn't right, my so-called intuition came out of nowhere. I was confused over the intense feelings I had. The thought of moving my island onto the mainland made me feel physically ill. I stayed silent and tried to make sense of my emotions. He continued to unpack, unaware of the evil that just entered our beautiful love story.

When I finally got to the shower, I let the unrelenting tears stream down my face until the last drop of hot water was gone. I was here, in a house with the man I've needed for so long, but I couldn't find any joy. I'd been waiting for this day for months, looking forward to our new life together, just to look in the mirror and find misery, the empty feeling of happiness evacuated. Over the next week, I tried to stay calm by drinking my weight in alcohol to help drown out the negative thoughts. Unable to mask my feelings any longer, I began to cry at the kitchen table.

He started to notice almost immediately as I continued to avoid the situation, searching for the right way to think, desperately trying to strike balance between logic and emotion. I turned to work for distraction, avoiding the horror story that was unfolding in front of me. Opening my balance sheet, I started to clean up and organize my books, the financial part of business that I was never good at. Running the numbers was quite possibly the worst thing I could have done at the time. Knowing what I know now, my PMDD symptoms were creating a negative emotional storm inside of me, blocking the possibility of any positive outlook. The lens that I looked through was so clouded by my own biology, I couldn't deal with anything even mildly challenging.

The long trip, lack of sleep and exercise combined with alcohol and eating like shit all helped trigger my undiagnosed PMDD. I silently unleashed a terrible, self-destructive monster. Unknowingly, I scoured through spreadsheets searching for my own failures, PMDD took over to provide evidence that I didn't deserve anything pleasant. I wasn't producing enough money to live on long term, no matter how I ran the numbers. My bank account was slowly being drained to make up for the difference between income and bills.

I had joked with him before, "If I fuck this up, you might have to pay all the rent for a while." He always agreed and we joked about it often. As I sat down in front of the balance sheet that day, I realized that this would be a reality. I might have to rely on him for a while. It was a pill I couldn't swallow in my fragile state, and I didn't feel like I deserved it.

I didn't deserve him, a man willing to move across the country to be with a poor single mother of two children. He didn't deserve to be with a woman who cried in the shower wondering if she was making the right decision. He took great care of his money; he didn't deserve to have his bank account suffer because of my inadequacy. Over the next week I proceeded to convince him that being with me was a mistake. I never asked him to help with my bills or discuss my financial concerns, PMDD did all the thinking and talking for me.

I convinced him that I was better off alone, I couldn't focus with him around and I had made a huge mistake. I was scared to death to tell him about my actual financial situation, embarrassed and ashamed of my failures. He attempted to understand what was happening, but I went in for the kill with every word, telling him that he wasn't ready to live in a house with me and my kids. He was collateral damage in a war that he knew nothing about. After a full week of turmoil, he packed up and left, retreating to his house without plans to return. The morning he drove away, he kissed me good-bye and was gone before I crawled out of bed, ready for a long drive back to Texas, sad and alone.

In the following weeks, unable to process and deal with what just happened, I switched all my energy to my business. Despite my hard work, my bank account continued to deplete, and I realized my business model wasn't sustainable. Expenses were crippling me, and I had no choice but to cut employees and start to work events myself. My ultimate mission was to work alone in isolation, an introvert's dream job. My dream moved to the backburner as I worked on keeping the bills paid. Working weddings was particularly difficult as I realized that marriage had come and gone for me. There would be no honeymoon, a lonely, poor divorcee in her thirties who couldn't seem to keep any relationship together.

Every weekend I was invited into someone else's special day, a fly on the wall witnessing people's happiest moments, unsure of what life had in store for me and if I'd ever be good enough to have a special celebration of my own. Surrounded by happy people, spending thousands of dollars on parties and weddings with huge families and countless friends, I began to shrink as I'd done so many times before.

My energy was drained quicker than my bank account, the tears rolled in when I least expected and forced me to stay in the bathroom just a bit longer to fix my makeup. The mood swings became more noticeable, remedied only by the open bars at events. Taking inventory of where I was, I realized that once again my hard work led me nowhere, it simply didn't serve me well.

Financially, I had catapulted myself back to where I was at seventeen, and this time I wasn't so sure I could dig myself out of it. My business was eating me alive financially and emotionally, the profits were nowhere near what I needed to maintain even a mediocre existence. The work itself was deteriorating to my soul and at the end of the day I was miserable, still single, and broke.

Reverse engineering is a process used by engineers, architects, and software developers to understand someone else's work. They use, study, and analyze programs to understand how they function. Studying and tracing information flow, they can start to map and piece together how a program works. The tool is used to compete with existing products or to replace old systems running on outdated technologies.

My relationship with money was certainly outdated, a flaw in my thinking that never served me well, a flaw that was easily exploited by PMDD. My business could have been successful, but until I solved the underlying issue within myself, any endeavor that I pursued would lead me to the same conclusion. My relationship could have worked but nothing beautiful is ever built from shame and guilt. I could have asked my boyfriend for help, he was great with money, but my shame—my ego—wouldn't allow it.

On any self-development journey, we must come to terms with the fact that we didn't create the first version of ourselves; our childhoods, experiences, and biology all played a role. Children aren't intentional about how they shape their own habits, and unfortunately most parents don't even know how to do it for themselves. Most of the world's people are not conscious of their own behaviors. They move on autopilot. They don't think about consequences and they are not intentional in their actions. They speak before they think. And it's all a product of who we believe ourselves to be, what we were raised to believe, and what our biology allows.

Reverse engineering yourself isn't a method of excuse but rather a path to explanation and improvement. My idea of never having enough was baked in, weaving itself into my thoughts and guiding my actions accordingly. Before we can get better, we need to start with where we are today and understand why we behave the way we do.

Financial security has plagued me since I was a small child. Despite my efforts I never seemed to find the right path out of hardship. It was as if I could never be released out of the continuous cycle of debt, poverty, and shame, and it was in part due to my own actions. My relationships suffered as a result, hiding my insecurities until they bubbled over, creating chaos and turmoil. Small choices throughout my life left me with little to show for my years of hard work. I was a thirty-three-year-old renter with no retirement plan or safety net. I'd sold my only asset just to save myself from myself and my habits were becoming recognizable, a pattern of self-destruction that I now considered to be a blatant affront to my attempts at survival and happiness.

I was stubborn, prideful, and I refused to ask anyone for help. I insisted on paying my part in every scenario, even to my own detriment. Regardless of how much money I made, I continued to live in lack. There was never enough, and I always needed more. Growing up in a poor, single-parent household, my relationship with money started out rough. We collected food stamps, got supplies from the food bank, our utilities were turned off. We were poor. My mother really did try, but she always seemed to struggle to earn a decent income. She took random low skilled jobs doing whatever she could to pay the bills. Our old gold-colored van had a broken window secured by a trash bag. I begged her to stop picking me up from school, I would walk instead.

The grocery store was embarrassing at times as she carefully chose what to put back after realizing that she couldn't afford everything in our cart. I felt her shame as a child, the same shame that would come back to haunt me for years afterwards, a feeling that was familiar and normal to me, a feeling that was baked into my unintentional version of life.

Looking back on when it all started, my deep-rooted relationship with money was that it was scarce, always. Every dollar that came in had to go back out. We always owed and never accumulated anything. We were always in debt to creditors threatening to take things away from us including the roof over our heads. As I progressed through life, my relationship with money stayed the same. Always trying to earn more but never focused on what I was doing with what I had.

As I sat back and analyzed my relationship with money, I realized that my perception of myself was to blame. I always felt poor regardless of how much I had, and until that changed, I would stay in the rat race eternally. I couldn't keep running my program the same way and expect success to just fall from the sky. I was nothing more than a product of a less than perfect environment, my unintentional version repeated my history in an endless loop. PMDD had free reign over my thoughts for a full week out of every month, and any insecurity was fair game for exploitation. Mental weaknesses that I didn't even know I had were magnified, forcing me to acknowledge them, forcing me to confront them.

What if instead of going through life on autopilot, we stopped just long enough to stand face to face with ourselves and stand up to the habits that no longer serve us? Instead of feeling like a failure, we can recognize that our first version was just a prototype to help us rebuild something fabulous. We are always just getting started, earlier versions only serve as a basis to build something extraordinary, a framework to help us improve on our own design.

What if for a moment we realize our discontent is nothing more than our own ability screaming at us, letting us know it's time to regroup? What if we stop and become so intentional that our habits, thoughts, and actions are created consciously rather than allowing silent forces to control us? My relationship with money was unhealthy, a toxic exchange with a narcissist that did nothing for me.

Promising myself I'd always have enough, I took inventory of my life. All our necessities were met, food was on the table, and we had a tiny roof over our head. We had enough today. Tomorrow we would wake up and have enough, every day was a new day to be intentional about having enough and being enough. I wouldn't compare myself to anyone else, my journey was not the same as theirs. I'd simply breathe, look around and discover that we had everything we needed, every day. A few pairs of shoes were more than enough, my car was enough, and my appearance was enough. Every meal was filled with gratitude. Remembering the days when I didn't have much choice, I realized that my past only defined my present and my future if I allowed it to. And I wasn't going to allow that to happen.

The idea of plenty radiated through me, infusing my thoughts with unwavering love for all that I had. I stopped feeling ashamed and guilty, my energy was refocused on my abundant life. I finally gave myself grace and allowed enough space for me to rebuild from the ground up. My next version would be carefully crafted with an abundant mind and unlimited potential, spreading love and hope by sharing my story. My story dedicated to those who suffer in silence at the mercy of their unintentional selves.

THROUGHPUT

"I have not failed, I have just found 10,000 ways that won't work."

(Thomas Edison)

Pushing ourselves in the wrong direction is like driving down the wrong side of the street; not only will we eventually crash, we will expend more energy than necessary trying to dodge traffic. The traffic flowing through our minds is incredibly unequal, and each person is unique in that aspect. What weighs me down might be exhilarating and energizing for someone else.

Capabilities are a double-edged sword because capability doesn't equal success, it doesn't equal greatness. Just because we can push through our pain, doesn't mean we're required to. Capabilities can run you into the ground and distract you from the reason you showed up in the first place. We oftentimes keep pushing through an uphill battle just for the sake of conquering a hill we don't even care about. Just because we *can* doesn't mean we *should*.

'Bandwidth' only refers to capacity, what we are capable of handling, what we *can* do. Bandwidth is theoretical, not actual and doesn't account for quality. How much can we download at any given time, how many movies can I stream in my house simultaneously? How many hours will this task take, how can I be more efficient, how can I create more time, how can I create more bandwidth? Does it count if our movies buffer every thirty seconds? Do we feel good about what we produce if it's subpar?

If we aren't concerned about the quality we bring into the world, we can go full throttle and use all our bandwidth to produce more shit. If we want to be great, however, we have to consider throughput; we have to measure actual success from point A to point B. Throughput is actual progress, it doesn't measure capacity, or what we are capable of rather it measures how much we produce successfully. Throughput varies from day to day and from person to person.

Regardless of what we are capable of we must determine our limitations, our wrong side of the road, the things that weigh us down, the things that decrease our chances of success. Instead of increasing bandwidth, which is inherently limited even if we were able to use our brain's full potential, we must pinpoint what increases our throughput. We must drive on our side of the road. What we can't see, we have to create.

As 2019 came to a close the event industry was in full swing and my business was in high demand. I was booked solid throughout the holiday season and I even turned customers away. At face value, this was a blessing, but the lessons were buried a few layers deeper when I finally realized I was driving directly into oncoming traffic.

The holidays kept me busy, running from myself wouldn't be difficult as I moved from party to party throughout the season. Some events were better than others, but every single one was draining and overstimulating for me. My only intent was to improve my quality of life, but I found myself in the middle of yet another downward spiral of despair.

Sitting alone in a busy Chick-Fil-A, I worked hard to fight back the tears so no one around me would notice my inner turmoil. With my mouth full of French fries, I thought to myself, *this is the worst day of my entire life*. It was a moment of hopelessness that radiated through every cell in my body. I can vividly remember looking down at my phone waiting to get a text back from my boyfriend. I missed him, and I wasn't doing well on my own. After he left, we stayed in touch and remained friends, even after I asked him to leave. We were hopeful that we could resurrect our love affair, we were still very much in love despite my emotional chaos.

My phone remained silent, the air around me seemed to grow heavy, and people buzzed around during lunch hour going about their day holiday shopping with loved ones. I stopped in to eat after leaving an event that didn't go as planned. After setting up a photo booth for a large corporate party, a cable broke, and my equipment wouldn't work. It was the simplest problem that could have been avoided had I been more prepared. Explaining to the host that I would have to issue a refund; I maintained my composure as she began to explain to the others in the room what was happening. It was a long walk back to my car and I'd have to make several trips back to the conference room to pack up my things before I could leave.

The event was starting, and everyone began to fill the room wearing ugly sweaters and reindeer antlers. Every trip back to the conference room was a chance to hear stories about the plans and hopes for the year to come, a happy, hopeful bunch of people ready to bring in the New Year. Hallways filled with corporate executives much like the ones that I used to sit in meetings with would pass me carrying equipment and let me know that the party was the other way. Politely explaining to everyone what had happened, I walked through the hallways of hell countless times until I was finally done.

I felt slightly nauseated. I was dazed and unsettled, feeling confused by what had just happened, even though a logical-thinking person could have clearly seen that it was an unforeseen incident for which I'd been ill-prepared. Disappointing and maybe embarrassing at worst. But to me, it was overwhelming. It was devastating.

My thoughts were exploding inside my head, and clearly, in hindsight, they were extreme given the situation. I drove only a short mile to the closest place to eat. I got out of my car, somehow managing to order food and sit down. Coming to terms with what just happened I tried to logically sort out how I felt. Looking around I realized how pitiful I had become—nothing more than a very lonely, very broken woman in what seemed to be a perpetual mid-life crisis.

Being surrounded by rich housewives with perfect skin and giant wedding rings I fantasized about what it would be like to be them. Spending the day shopping for Christmas gifts, returning home to a beautiful house with a husband who helped them carry their bags inside. Unable to hold back the tears any longer, I peeled myself out of the chair, grabbed my food and left in a hurry to avoid anyone noticing my mid-day sob fest. When I got to my car, the tears started to roll down my cheeks, a familiar sensation that I had grown accustomed to over the years.

My drive home was a chance to further piece together my own thoughts and feelings, attempting to make sense of where I was emotionally. Unable to find any sense of grounding, I felt out of control. Driving my Toyota filled with party equipment, I envisioned what my wreck site might look like. I thought about the holiday props strewn about the highway next to the woman who finally found relief.

Not knowing how I got there, I pulled into the driveway of my tiny apartment complex, pouring a drink before unloading my equipment into the living room. Searching through my phone once again, there was still no reply. Back to back parties meant little time to recover and recharge from each event. I was in constant overdrive, an overstimulated, emotionally disturbed train wreck that was slowly dying inside. Bottled up emotion began to seep out unchecked but not undetected, guiding me towards bad behaviors with deep consequences.

The corporate event may have gone terribly wrong, but the one before it took the cake. A few days prior I was scheduled to work a pub crawl in the heart of the Indianapolis bar scene, a small village called Broad Ripple. Drunk people came in droves, spilling beer on me, attempting to hold long, slurred conversations before moving onto the next bar. After hours of being on my feet, I finally ordered a double rum and coke to help get me through the rest of the night.

Looking down at my phone, surrounded by stumbling co-eds, I see a text from my boyfriend that triggered a burning rage inside of me. I had spent the previous month apologizing and begging him to come back, writing novels through text messaging and telling him how sorry I was for what happened and how I acted. I did everything I could to work things out, spending countless hours writing, begging, and pleading for him to forgive me. Despite my efforts, he wouldn't budge. He would wait it out from afar so that we could have some time apart.

Moving back to Texas, he pulled up to his house and resumed his old way of life, the barbeque sauce was still in the fridge, right where he left it, a tiny detail that stuck out in my mind, making me question if he really wanted to move in the first place. His friends and family were close by for companionship and support through his 'rough breakup'. That night, as I stood in a puddle of spilled beer, he sent me a picture of guacamole that he made. He'd spent his Saturday with friends cooking, living his usual uninterrupted, peaceful, perfect life.

Exhausted, overwhelmed and feeling defeated, the picture ignited an unavoidable, inevitable fire inside of me. This wasn't the fire used to light up a room but rather the one used to burn the house down. Hell week was back, and I was filled with pure rage, and my emotional responses were directed right at him. Infuriated, I was reminded of how easy his life had returned to normal while mine continued to spiral downhill. Without an emotional escape route, I grabbed another double from the bar and proceeded to do my job.

Struggling through the large crowd, the guy at the bar and the bouncer both had eyes on a troubled woman, keeping her cool despite the spilled beer and stumbling crowd. She had black framed glasses and her dark hair fell to the small of her back, with a few bouncing curls at the end. While the bouncer attempted to play his role as the protector of the damsel in distress, the guy at the bar swooped in for the kill. He and his friends introduced themselves, a clean-cut group of pharmacists that worked at the hospital nearby. Boldly, he asked me to have a drink with him afterwards, an offer I couldn't refuse in my current state. With a serotonin disruption, rum flowing through my veins, and a boyfriend who didn't seem to care how I was faring, I was wide open to having a much better night.

After the event, the bouncer insisted on helping me to my car, undoubtedly so he could watch me walk past, my jeans hugging my body as if every inch of the denim was made just for me. After packing up my equipment, I met the pharmacist at a nearby hole-in-the-wall bar. After an hour of chatting and realizing how late it was getting, we moved the party back to his house. Ignoring my phone, texts from my boyfriend asking if I'd made it home went unanswered; all his calls went to voicemail. The pharmacist leaned in and grabbed my hips, pulling me closer as he started kissing me.

Clinging on to what felt like the last fiber of my morals, I told him goodnight and headed home. Melting into my couch cushions, I was exhausted from the entire experience and at odds with myself and my choices. Facing my boyfriend the next day, I told him what happened; all the time I'd spent trying to work things out seemed futile. I had finally given up on him and any chance of reigniting our love affair.

The events slowed down just in time for Christmas and presents filled the space under my tiny tree. While my daughter visited family back home in Texas, my son and I had a quiet celebration filled with toys. Gifts were the one thing I always provided regardless of my hardships. I put on a fake smile but all I wanted was to be alone, to be in my own space, attempting to understand and reflect on the year passed. I knew that I had to get better, I knew my children deserved more from me; I knew I had to change. With the season coming to an end I finally found a glimmer of peace, quiet, and stillness to curl into a corner and start to lick my wounds.

Leaning into my troubled mind and realizing that suicidal thoughts were becoming a dangerous part of my life, I started Googling "suicidal thoughts in women" and stumbled across PMDD online. Watching first-hand accounts on YouTube was like listening to myself talk; hearing other women describe the feelings and sensations of hell week made me realize that I was not alone in my struggle. I made an appointment with my gynecologist, the one specialist that I had never discussed my symptoms with before. After twenty years of ups and downs, silently battling on my own, I finally received a proper diagnosis.

I analyzed symptoms and read the tragic story of Gia Allemand, who gave her precious life to the disorder. The *Bachelor* star that seemed to have everything, lost her grueling battle with PMDD. She finally escaped her misery by hanging herself in her home with a vacuum cord.

I felt her despair, I saw where she was, and I knew exactly why she did it. I was teetering on the same edge that she walked before me. She was young, beautiful, and talented, she had everything a girl like me could dream of, but PMDD showed no mercy. Far away from the spotlight sitting in my living room in yoga pants, I felt connected to her, we were more alike than we were different, suffering from the same mental anguish, fighting the same silent invisible battle. After twenty years, I had finally connected the dots of my deeply troubled life.

My diagnosis was bittersweet. While I started to understand myself better, I was left with the realization that I had limitations, I couldn't be like everyone else. I couldn't be as consistent as I wanted, I felt less capable and somehow more fearful of the future. My bandwidth was reduced. I felt like I would never be able to do as much as other women could. I felt like I couldn't do what the average man could. After living a life on full throttle, I was forced to slow down, I was forced to accept that I had to rest, I had to eat well, and I couldn't skip my workouts. I had to avoid high stress environments and the alcohol had to be reduced. I had to take time to do things I *enjoyed* to relieve stress.

This way of living was foreign to me. Rather than doing things I liked, I was usually spinning my wheels doing things that I *thought* I should be doing. Working, improving, cooking, cleaning, attempting to fix my countless fuck ups in life. Realizing I had absolutely no hobbies, I had to create one. A few days after my diagnosis I opened my laptop and started writing, something I enjoyed but never did for fun. I didn't know what I'd write about, my mind swarmed with ideas from childhood, my journey as an entrepreneur, my inability to have meaningful long-term relationships, and my endless epic failures.

My writing was terrible at first, a jumbled mixture of ideas that didn't make sense. The paragraphs resembled the artwork of a two-year-old, cans of paint thrown at a canvas, pure chaos. Regardless of the output, the *process* was freeing. All the ideas in my head suddenly had a destination. I could say and do whatever I wanted; I could use the word 'unfuck' as a verb. There were no limitations here, no judges, and no consequences for doing it "wrong". I was driving on my own side of the road. No, I was driving on the road I built myself. And there were no traffic cops, no thought police. I could go as fast or as slow as I wanted. I could stop in the middle of the street and put it in reverse. My bandwidth may have decreased, but my throughput multiplied exponentially.

VALUES MAPPING

"All of humanity's problems stem from man's inability to sit quietly in a room alone."

(Pascal)

Individual personal values can be defined as what you show up for and how you show up. They drive your needs and what is important to you as a person. Examples range from creativity to achievement to humility and self-awareness; the list is limited only by the words used to describe them. Everyone has a set of personal values, and whether they are consciously aware of them or not, values run our lives behind the scenes.

When we are well aligned with those values, we have a sense of well-being and wholeness. When we live at odds with who we are, who we're becoming, or who we're meant to be, negativity begins to brew inside of us, bubbling over and stifling our growth. As with most transformative experiences, it takes being pushed so far out of your own comfort zone to even begin to understand what your values are.

For me and so many others, 2020 was supposed to be the year of great hope and improvement, a year of change. The economy was doing well, and unemployment was down, many Americans were hopeful for a prosperous future. New Years was right around the corner, the PMDD trance faded away and the light at the end of the tunnel shined brighter than ever before as I realized there was hope. I wasn't crazy, well maybe a little but I could finally begin to understand myself and that seemed like enough. I was excited to be my own research subject and analyze myself back into wholeness. I vowed to make 2020 my best year, I would right all my wrongs and learn how to love myself especially in my 25%. I refused to lose myself to my other self and I promised to do everything in my power to get better.

First things first—it was time to get rid of the business that no longer served me. I could have fixed my financial problems and reduced my expenses to make it more lucrative but at the end of the day the work didn't bring me joy and I refused to spend any of my 75% doing work that I hated. Being around crowds of people, forced to socialize, refrain from cursing, and wearing anything other than yoga pants was too much for me—for the new spirit that longed to emerge. In January 2020, I sold the business for enough money to pay rent for the year at my small apartment complex.

Unknowingly I made one of the best financial decisions of my life as the virus was silently spreading itself across the globe getting ready to put millions of small business owners out of work. My daughter stayed in Texas for a while longer to spend much needed time with her father and I asked my ex-husband to keep my son during hell week so I could care for myself. I asked for help in every form available without guilt or hesitation. I studied my disorder and myself and found the Yoga with Adriene YouTube channel to help soothe my body and my soul.

Through meditation and visualization, I started piecing together what my next version should be, a much happier woman tuned into her own innate ability, a master of her craft. I discovered psilocybin and the woman in the basement and most importantly I kept writing. While my life was stabilizing, it was a tragic thought that it took a diagnosed mental disorder for me to get there. But often, beauty forms in response to a wound.

PMDD gave me justification for things that everyone should have—peace within themselves, and the opportunity to heal. More importantly, PMDD allowed me to be unwell at times, a very normal part of human existence. With the idea that it was perfectly ok to be imperfect, the world presented itself in a new light. Instead of worrying about fixing my 25%, I started focusing on how I could be the happiest version of myself, 75% of the time.

Little did I know, the world would begin to deal out hands from a completely different deck and the game of life was about to get interesting. 2020 marked the beginning of a historical event that would force millions of people to make tough decisions in a time of great uncertainty. My individual journey would continue in parallel to this as hell year began to unfold, an invisible battle with biology that pushed the world off balance. If there was anything that PMDD taught me it was that biology is much more powerful than we give it credit for and change is inevitable, both good and bad.

Without a vaccine, the best weapon we had was sending people home to isolate from the world. For many, the quarantine was a ruthless test of whether they could abstain from human connection and remain sane. For me, it was a chance to understand that solitude was the only path to consider going forward. I required alone time to think, reflect and continue exploring myself and my own abilities. So many of us dangerously live in extreme extraversion, intertwined with others' thoughts and ideas, effectively drowning out our own brilliance. But now, even a hug was off limits.

Uncomfortable at first, loneliness sets in to remind us of our dependence on others, hijacking our focus and attempting to redirect our path back to what our mind believes to be normal. Leaning into discomfort, the other side of solitude is clarity into ourselves that can only be understood in a room alone. The world was not just at war with a deadly virus, we were also at war with forced isolation. Some people spiraled into loneliness while others explored a life of being alone, wondering how they'd missed out on this peaceful opportunity all these years. But regardless of how each of us reacted to the new normal, everyone involuntarily got quiet enough to hear their soul speak.

Time spent reflecting into wholeness and awareness is the exact prescription required to follow your own inner greatness, those voices held deep inside of a person, some screaming to get out, others just a still small voice that won't go away. Undoubtedly, the hell year that was thrust upon us without warning would expose great tragedy and silver linings as we began to navigate a new environment with fresh perspectives. What once seemed important was moved to the back burner as many lost their livelihoods, and others lost their loved ones. We were all forced to reconsider our values and prioritize what was most important.

Uncertain times call for certainty in values. There was nowhere to hide from yourself. As the virus raged on, quarantines became harder to control; some people grew desperate to move on with their life and go back to normal. Projections and ideas for solutions ranged widely across scientific communities, political and socio-economic divides.

Small individual decisions made during this time placed individuals' values in full view, as if they were stamped on people's foreheads. You didn't have to protest or post on social media to make people aware of what you believed in. Everyone's actions were being watched under a microscope.

Basic human nature urges us to look towards others for guidance, to spot social norms and fit into the groups that we associate with. Following the wrong group and making the wrong call in this scenario could have easily led us down a path that we didn't fully sign up for.

This was a time of great individualism, every person reacting to the situation just a bit differently according to their own values system. Happiness would fade away for many, depression and anxiety taking its place as they lived outside of their comfort zone, feeling trapped and unaligned, unsure of what to do. For some, fear of losing their livelihoods, and possibly everything they owned as a result, would be at the top of the list. For those who continued to work on the front lines, face to face with the virus, from healthcare workers to grocery store employees and other essential services, they had more deadly concerns. Among the army of people who risked their lives to help others, happiness varied accordingly.

For many, including myself, these were defining moments that showed us what we were all about, quiet solitude surrounded by chaos and destruction, living in slow motion not knowing what the outcome would be.

So, the first steps to my rewrite was erasing bad habits and predetermined ideas, but after that I was left with a void that I wasn't quite prepared for. If I was no longer bothered by the basic social norms of society, I'd have to dig deep to determine who I was and what I stood for.

Muting the outside world, I began to feel connected to who I was, graciously accepting the mission that I signed up for; sharing my story for those who desperately needed to hear it. Turning my despair into inspiration and hope for millions of women who wanted to dig themselves out of the trenches.

Oftentimes, we start self-improvement journeys with a particular goal in mind. We want to accomplish something concrete, attainable, and defined. As I sat down to understand what made me happy, I realized that happiness is not a goal, it's just a state of being. I could move in and out of it and just like anything else, it would change with time. It's not like a degree or a sum of money, it's intangible. You can't see it, hold it, touch it, or hang it on your wall. Unlike an achievement, you can be happy and then not happy. It's something that evolves. When we think of a happy person, we just see someone who's happy more often than not.

A happy person's autopilot redirects them when something pushes them off course, recovering quickly like a missile locked on to a target. For me, happiness would need to be conditioned, I had to work on it over time, but first I had to define it for myself. To say we just want to be happy is vague and lacks individualized meaning. Starting with semantics, I selected a more appropriate word: well-being.

The dictionary defines well-being as "a good or satisfactory condition of existence; a state characterized by health, happiness, and prosperity; welfare."

Like many people I struggled with what well-being looked like for me. Without many references from childhood, how could one determine well-being? I had the definition, but it was still vague in the context of my life.

Oftentimes, it's easier for us to understand the definition of a word by studying what it is not. The antonym that stuck out to me the most was *danger*. If I couldn't define well-being, I could define the things that felt dangerous. The exercise got incredibly easier; I could make a list of my biggest fears much faster than defining my happiness. The key to this exercise was in the conscious, intentional, critical thinking of what was dangerous for me. Our fears are driven by underlying thoughts that take on a mind of their own without intention or direction guiding our actions. Had I left it up to my old unintentional version, I would have continued to live in fear of being poor, although I realized over time that being poor was still plenty.

My old version would have feared not achieving enough and ending up lonely, but none of that seemed to matter anymore. Fear is part of our life, and it reveals a lot about where we are if we stop long enough to look at it. My old fears weren't relevant anymore, they seemed to evolve along my journey. My values followed suit, transforming into a set of meaningful words that helped guide me through the next chapter of my life. With thought and consideration, I came up with my top three fears. Next to each fear, I added the most appropriate antonym to represent my values.

Figure 1. Values Mapping

FEAR	VALUE
Unaware	Self-Awareness
Collectivity	Individualism
Society	Solitude

The words that I landed on were not what I expected when I started the exercise. The top three that made the cut were aligned to where I needed to be for the next stage of my growth. They weren't a generic list like honesty, work ethic, and responsibility. The basics are covered by a baseline moral compass that everyone has to some degree, and I feel like they are constants vs meaningful personal values.

The list wasn't a set of deep-rooted values from my past experiences or a list I found online. Rather they were guided by intention for my own progression. The most dangerous thing for me was not knowing myself, not paying enough attention to where I was and not understanding the complexity of my own mind. My most prized possession and my most powerful weapon needed direction and constant oversight because without it, biology would continue to hold me hostage whereas self-awareness would keep me and my loved ones safe from myself.

Celebrating my individuality and the silver linings that showed up for me, I shuddered at the idea of collective thinking, and leaned into my own thoughts instead. Understanding more about myself through the previous chapters in this book, I knew that spending too much time with groups of people overwhelmed me. My next phase would be a journey of solitude. I had to detach from others' ideas to form my own. I had to drive alone before I allowed anyone to travel on my highway.

My biggest fears would have easily hindered my transformational journey had I ignored them and let them dilute the emergent, authentically raw version of myself. In the quiet, we can tune into our fears and let them shine the light on what we need to pay attention to, the values that we must hold onto, regardless of the risk.

Halfway through this book, I started thinking about how others may perceive my writing and whether or not they would find value in it, and I started to doubt myself. Those fears were innate and unconscious, simple leftovers from my environment that had conditioned me over the years to believe them even if that fear was unfounded for my present—for what was happening right now—and for my future. Always bringing myself back to awareness, I removed any extra fears that didn't make my list from the equation. Self-doubt would have to wait; the book would persist despite it.

2020 was a year of great change, a chance for transformation not available in the status quo. People suffered and struggled; the lens of their life clouded by a small piece of nature. Faced with new threats, fears evolved, and values changed. Individual personal journeys like my own would continue in parallel creating complexity in how we managed the next chapter of our lives. The underlying presumption that everyone wanted to go back to normal incorrectly assumed that normal had equaled happiness for the masses.

The virus had a way of forcing some people to reshuffle the hands dealt to them and reconsider whether their pre-virus lives were worth returning to. As the world started to open again, the harsh reality was that some people would dread the idea of returning back to their previous way of life, some scared of the virus, others scared of continuing to live a life they hated. Every story would be just a bit different and every moment of despair would one day create the opposite reaction because hope is baked into who we are, humanity simply wouldn't exist without it. Hope is the human spirit. Underneath layers of serotonin and hope, the desire to end the pain and suffering exists in all of us.

Every month after hell week is over, I pick up the pieces and grow, learning just a little bit more about myself and my values through the process, I make necessary changes to make my life better. On a much larger scale, the world was lit up with change, disrupted by biology, and we would all be forced to take a long hard look in the mirror during hell year. Lessons learned in these intimate, private moments would serve as the building blocks of change for the next beautiful 75%.

AGILE SELF-DEVELOPMENT

"As the water shapes itself to the vessel that contains it, a wise man should adapt himself to circumstances"

(Confucius)

C hanging the way we think, and act is a key component of growth, but oftentimes we cower in the face of change as if it's the enemy sent to overthrow our kingdom. Planning, while necessary to an extent, can derail our ambitions by allowing our unintentional versions plenty of time to talk us out of our own amazing ideas. Meanwhile, small windows of opportunity can close right in front of our faces while we sit back and debate with ourselves.

There was no better time than 2020 to chart a new course. The world was blooming with opportunities for people who interpreted the situation as such. Dead ends can lead us to new beginnings, new encounters, and more enriching experiences. In trying times, finding silver linings requires only a little more effort than succumbing to negativity. Change is constant and inevitable, both within us and in our environments. Self-development can be hard, a grueling test of our discipline and patience. Throw in an ever-changing and unpredictable environment and we can easily get knocked off course before we even get started.

The reality is that we change every single day whether we know it or not. Our skin wrinkles just a bit more than the day before, grey hairs become more plentiful and every cell in our body grows one day older. We are a walking, talking, vehicle of change. Green leaves turn to red and gold, snow covers the grass and eventually the birds come out to sing once again; change surrounds us in everything that we do and everything that we know.

The idea that we will always struggle, never able to break the chains we've put ourselves in, goes against everything that we are as humans. We are ever evolving and ever adapting, adjusting to change daily on a biological and unconscious level. Or we're creating intentional, conscious change, the kind that really serves us well, and this is the most difficult, requiring more complex effort. It is oftentimes met with resistance from ourselves and others. But creative, conscious change comes from a place of inspiration. It's a natural part of existence when we learn to let go of resistance, fear, and the conventional parameters society has placed on us.

The decision to give up everything did not come easy. Quitting my job, selling my house, moving across the country, buying, and selling a business all in the middle of a battle with my mental health was hard. As a necessary part of my growth, I'd do it again if doing the opposite meant never changing, never breaking through my own barriers to live a beautiful, purpose-driven life. Falling in love after a divorce and then losing it was heartbreaking, but it was worth every second of the pain. Without my tragic love affair, it may have taken much longer to find my diagnosis.

Had I known about my disorder earlier on, I would have approached the situation differently. I would have gotten help instead of constantly running from my feelings. I could have looked back with regret realizing that the last twenty years of my life were spent in needless turmoil, but that thought didn't serve me well. I'd given up too much of my life already to live my next chapter in regret. No one gets a playbook for life and there's dignity in the struggle regardless of how unfair it seems.

My life wasn't meant for comfort and ease; stability and security would be among the most difficult things for me to achieve. Just as soon as I thought I was getting somewhere I'd be knocked off course again by my own ovaries; biology forced me to live in constant, unconscious change.

Stability and security are nice sounding words, but the reality is that they are usually feelings rather than environments. In the modern age, we are long past the days of fighting lions on the Sahara, but the parts of our brain that react to stress remain mostly the same. Fight or flight ruled my life for years, my stress levels were elevated most of the time, and I was a walking talking, beautiful, hot, fucking mess.

I'd never felt secure in a relationship, a job, a home or in my own abilities, but that was the very reason why I continued to evolve and grow. I learned to value self-awareness over outward signs of security and stability. Getting quiet and looking inward, I found that I could create my own sense of stability while taking major risks to get better and live better. Just having my feet firmly planted on the earth is a positive feeling if I leaned into it for a moment. In those intentional, present moments, I was reassured that I had a place here, I could connect to something much larger than myself. Rather than feeling the earth beneath our feet, we often turn to our bank account or the house we live in to reassure us and help us feel safe. Fragility is baked into security granted from the outside world, holding us against our will at the mercy of a constantly changing environment and the minutes on a clock.

The virus caused plenty of turbulence to everyday life. Supply chains were disrupted, and store shelves were wiped out faster than they could be restocked. Groceries weren't the only thing that was in short supply. My mushroom stash was depleting quickly. My supplier stopped growing to focus on more important activities in his life. After finding a remarkable treatment for my symptoms, I suddenly lost access to it.

There's no evidence for psychological addiction or physical dependence on psilocybin, and there are no withdrawal symptoms when it leaves your body. The difficulty for me was not addiction, but rather finding a replacement coping mechanism or figuring out how to grow them myself. My doctor was out of reach except for cases of emergency, which for me could literally be every month if I wasn't able to pull myself together.

It was hell week again. Schools were closed, I was running out of money and I couldn't find toilet paper anywhere. To say I'd have to rise to the occasion was an understatement. Emotionally I was in a weird place. Months into my self-development journey I lost my sense of grounding, I was thrown off course by the situation. Going back to my values, I had to maintain self-awareness at all costs. I was more deadly to myself than any virus could ever be if I didn't pay attention to where I was. First things first, if the world was coming to an end, I was at least going to eat the rest of my mushrooms. I carved out a day to be alone to regroup and gather my thoughts. I had enough left for one microdose; it would have to be enough for the foreseeable future. With my dog by my side, we headed outside for a long run to clear my mind.

After my stint in the Army, I had let go of keeping track of miles or pace, I just ran until my heart no longer fluttered from anxiety. I ran until I had control over my breath, until I could take a breath so deep that I finally felt the calmness flow through my body. Over the years I developed an addiction to the runner's high, so much so that I'd keep pushing long after I felt my muscles starting to tremble. My dedication to exercise seemed obsessive but it was never about the way I looked. I'd known for years, deep down inside, it helped to keep me sane.

Feeling the slight euphoria of the microdose and focused breathing, I took in the beauty of everything around me. The tall trees overhead, the bright green grass, and the feeling of the open air on my skin was delightfully refreshing. In nature, I felt a sense of being ridiculously small, miniscule in the grand scheme of things. This feeling wasn't a bad thing, rather it was humbling to consider the vastness of the world around me. My problems, worries, and doubts seemed even smaller, tiny figments of my own imagination. The pavement and dirt roads were unlimited, I never felt boxed in or trapped. There was always another direction, always another path.

I'd lost access to my self-medication but not my drive or newfound sense of self. The show must go on, the project couldn't be swayed by anyone or anything. Refocusing, I brought the woman in the basement back through repetitive meditation and visualization, no drugs required. I worked out as much as possible, allowing the natural processes of endorphins to do their magic. Continuing with my writing, I had to remain grounded in what I was doing, I couldn't allow the uneasiness of the world to steal my focus.

My only plan was to continue to do what served me well, so I just kept writing. My work was all over the place. I went back, read it out loud, revised and edited until even the monster inside of me was happy and content. I could worry about my future later regardless of how incredibly wobbly I felt at times. I knew I had to get the words out of me before I could move on. My visualizations were focused, the woman, a master of her craft, studied each line of code, carefully selecting only the most important.

She was a brilliant programmer; she not only knew how to write the code I required but also how to prioritize what was most important. She welcomed change and uncertain environments into her work, she was adaptive and agile. The work performed was important, but the work not performed was celebrated. Writing too many lines of code and becoming too much too fast was a fool's errand, we couldn't conquer the world and we didn't try. Small iterations were the name of the game, over planning and over analyzing had no seat at my table. The biggest project of my life was underway in the middle of chaos and uncertainty, but I'd find opportunity rather than despair and depression.

Looking back at my experience at a small software company, I learned a thing or two about the process. The reality is that over half of all software development projects fail miserably. Traditionally, software development focused on planning every detail before the project ever started. The focus was on planning rather than agility and adaptation.

Over time, large projects became difficult to adapt and overcome changes to the original plans. While competition, regulation, and other factors continually evolved, software development struggled to keep pace. Inflexible techniques would continue to cripple multi-million-dollar projects until the industry found a better way to deliver value. In response to faster moving business climates, agility was built into the process. Agile software development began replacing archaic practices and change was no longer a threat, it was welcomed and expected.

Self-development projects on the other hand, fail at an even higher rate for the same reasons. We've all been there, from the gym membership that goes unused to never leaving the job we hate, we fail on an epic level. The moment we have a goal in mind, we are optimistic, and ready to take on the world, but any little thing can throw us off track.

Just like the archaic principles of the software development industry, we don't prepare ourselves for adaptation. Instead we set rigid goals at the beginning of our journey and create inflexible plans that force us to declare failure when any little thing goes wrong. We drill a definition of success into our heads without leaving enough room for our ever-changing environments. Every one of us is a multi-million-dollar endeavor, we are too big to fail, and our own individual improvement process should weave in agility or flexibility, increasing our chance for success.

Writing became part of my self-care routine, and unlike anything I had ever done, it got better during hell week. The words I couldn't seem to find suddenly appeared with deep, unfiltered emotion. Increased self-criticism forced me to revisit and re-edit, the work took on a mind of its own and my disorder added fuel to the beautiful fire. I wasn't writing a story; I wasn't telling a story. I was submersed in a world that was unfolding before me.

My idea of work began to change, opportunity began to present itself, and it was time for me to adapt to a new way of thinking. My skills in technology were solid, a stable industry that could provide security, but it wasn't fulfilling or forgiving for a woman with a mental health disorder.

After twenty years of running from myself I found peace and satisfaction in writing, it was my thing, it gave me purpose. I knew that I was not alone in my journey, there were women before me who suffered in silence and there would be women after me, desperate to find refuge from their own beautiful minds. Like Gia, there would be some that would give their lives to PMDD. Troubled teenagers would run away from themselves before even knowing who they were. They would navigate the same struggles that I became intimately familiar with.

Families would go without answers, losing their loved ones to a widely misunderstood part of biology. Women around the world would be left to their own devices in a cruel landscape, trying to keep their head above water, just trying to survive from one hour to the next. The woman in the basement would never fully escape for some of them, the sounds of their heels would fade away, talents that could have been perfected by their inner drive to do better and get better would not see the light of day, and their compassion and understanding for others would go unexplored as they hid from the world.

The silver linings of their despair wouldn't be apparent, they'd be clouded by suicidal thoughts and an ever-decreasing deficit of self-worth. I couldn't be there to catch those who have fallen, and I can't be there to catch those who will yet fall, but I can write for each and every one of them. I can write until I—until we—leave our mark on the world, until people across nations know of our secret tribe of women.

Rising to the occasion, adapting to circumstances, the only question I had was how I could make it happen, never allowing thoughts of how I might fail.

INPUT VALIDATION

"This is simply amazing. I'm in tears right now, yet so inspired by you. Please keep writing."

(Mandeh M.)

So comes the day when there's no turning back. When I would finally expose my true colors to the world and graciously ask for acceptance from myself and others. Imperfections and troubled thoughts that were so desperately hidden became the very method I used to connect with other beautiful minds. The auto pilot that was once locked onto failure, mediocrity, and distress began to change course, narrowing in on the dream destinations of my future. Rather than holding me back, my program began to serve me well, finally making good decisions on my behalf.

Information was carefully filtered and validated before reaching the beautiful work of art that I designed within myself. I noticed the difference in my perception; red flags arose as information contrary to my self-image presented itself. The ideas that I may not be strong enough, good enough, pretty enough, or smart enough were replaced with only one question; am I *me* enough?

My gifts for the world would appear on center stage, showcasing the details I'd been missing my entire life, the heart that bled for all the world to see. All vulnerabilities and strengths exposed. My filter became so powerful that the noise that used to overwhelm me was muted and I heard the joyous frequency of my own song vibrating like the soft flutter of wings, playing in my own mind, a symphony and a choir at once, a well-orchestrated and intensely focused *hum*.

Goosebumps covered my skin.

The room lights up when I walk in now. My greatness spills over for others to enjoy. I am no longer a burden on my society of one, but a contributor to the potential happiness of myself and others. Yet I am authentically me, without pride or prejudice, without judgment or fear.

Despite our rocky relationship, unknowingly, my mother taught me one of the most valuable lessons in life. She showed me what it's like to live a life ignoring talent, distracted by the weakness of her 25%. Growing up I learned more about art than most kids, especially poor kids who were not well traveled. Picasso, Rembrandt, and Kandinsky were household names, and acrylic paints, charcoal, and canvases lined every closet in our small home. The TV played *Six Degrees of Separation* more times than I could count. The 1996 film starring Will Smith showcased a rare double-sided Kandinsky; the line "Chaos, Control" still rings out in my mind.

Art was the only thing my mother ever talked about, it was the one thing that made her eyes light up, it was the one thing that she could focus on. She would stand in awe in front of paintings, her head in the clouds, connecting to the artist beneath the work. Regardless of where life took her, she was an artist, always has been and always will be.

Growing up, she was one of five children that my grandmother raised on her own in a rough part of town. My grandma, who meant well, picked their family home only because it was zoned into the richer school district, with the hope of giving her kids a brighter future than she had. My mother's tanned skin and dark hair stuck out in the hallways full of blue-eyed blondes. To make things even more interesting, she was academically challenged and struggled with ADD, although she wouldn't be diagnosed until years later.

Simple math was foreign to her, reading and writing was a constant challenge, and to this day, she struggles to spell simple words. Barely scraping by throughout high school, just graduating would be difficult. At sixteen, she landed a job at a theme park, drawing caricatures for the crowds, her head in the clouds, dreaming that one day, she too, would have her artwork proudly displayed in a gallery.

After graduating, she headed to college with only one goal: to become an artist. Out of all her siblings, she was the only one who would attempt to go to college, but it would prove to be a short lived pursuit to chase her dreams and live a life with her head in the clouds. After a year, humbled by life and faced with financial hardship, she put her dreams on hold. She needed more money to pay tuition and buy art supplies. Coming from a poor family, there was no help, no one to fall back on financially.

Military recruitment ads scattered throughout campus prompted her to visit the nearest Army recruiting station where she signed away four years of her life in exchange for college money. What was intended to be a simple break from her dreams turned into thirty years of attempting to live as someone else; her greatness would be put on hold for far too long. Marriage, children, divorce, and remarriage followed by becoming a widow would consume her. Failed attempts at becoming good at things like reading, writing, and math to find work would define far too many years of her life.

Lost in books, I was an oddball in her house full of coloring, painting, and trips to art museums. The written word had appealed to me from an incredibly young age, and my mother often turned to me for help with writing and spelling. Her disorganized aloofness and the way she scribbled lists in circles was odd to me. She seemed quite different from the other parents in the neighborhood. She forgot everything, including where and when to pick me up at times. Budgeting was non-existent, oftentimes overdrawing her bank account and forgetting to pay bills. Water and electricity would be shut off from time to time, sometimes because of a lack of money, sometimes because she didn't realize the bill was due a few weeks prior.

She rarely cooked, instead getting lost in TV shows after work. Our home was usually cluttered chaos with piles of laundry strewn about and dishes in the sink. When I got older, I wondered if she may have had a closet drug problem because nothing about her life made sense. To me, it seemed impossible to mess up simple tasks as much as she did. As vanilla as they come, she never dabbled in mind altering substances and I remember her drinking only a handful of times.

It wasn't until much later, after my own struggle through life, that I realized that her condition was due to living at odds with her own 25%. Running a household and working jobs that required her to be organized and timely weighed on her over the years, and each year grew harder than the one before. She always seemed to be struggling.

There was little time for art and her head was pulled far from the clouds into a more mediocre existence. The way she spoke of herself was more aligned with her failures than her talents. Always trying to improve, she worked at finishing college on and off throughout the years, always struggling with English and math. She spent countless hours with tutors and ended up taking the classes more than once. Her artwork would become a distant reality, collecting dust rather than being displayed for others to enjoy. For years, her 75% was hidden, stuffed away, in a futile effort to improve her 25%, but her inner voice never died. The artist inside of her finally found a way out when she became an art teacher in her 50's, an advocate for kids who had raw talent but didn't perform well in core subjects.

When I was at odds with my work, I'd always look back on my mother's life as an artist. The artist who doesn't make art, the engineer who never tinkers, and the musician who never makes music rob the world of their fresh perspectives, their enriching creativity, and their innovation. In the day and age of improving weaknesses we have a way of forgetting our strengths. Much like our values, it can be hard to figure out what they are, but we do know what they aren't. Throughout my career I figured that I would need to stay in tech, it was a strong industry and there was plenty of room to grow.

My master's in information systems would serve me well, or so the research told me. The single fundamental flaw in my plan was that I didn't research myself first. Through college, I'd get through my classes just fine, an average student that wrote twenty-page papers like they were nothing. The average student with a keen eye for semantics and creative writing, even in technical subjects. Becoming a writer or a creative type never crossed my mind, because surely it would confine me to a life like my mother's, or so I thought at the time.

When I began to write this book, in the middle of despair, it was like finally finding a key to the locked away version of myself. The young child who got lost in books; the toddler who demanded to learn more was unleashed back into the world. A reincarnation of my drive after my diagnosis, that child was reckless, careless, and unforgiving in her pursuit to continue doing what she loved. Defiant, rebellious, and tenacious, I felt alive again. I felt like the fifteen-year girl who escaped the hallways of hell and was spending time with friends in a garage, properly self-medicating. I felt like the person I was before I wanted to die.

Spending time on myself throughout the first chapters in this book paved the way for new ideas about work. Coming to terms with my 75% uptime, I longed to create a life that would just allow me to be unwell at times. Forced to spend countless hours in meetings would be a dangerous endeavor because undoubtedly there would come a time when I would actually burst into tears in a conference room.

There would come a time when I reenacted the scene from *Half Baked* where the guy working at the burger place walked out of his job. Before leaving, I'd grab the intercom and yell "Fuck you, fuck you, fuck you, you're cool, fuck you, I'm out." The scene played out far more often in my mind than a normal human and I think my facial expressions printed the thoughts on my forehead.

During hell week, I was emotionally disturbed and brutally honest; holding back in a professional setting became nearly impossible. Though I'd somehow managed to do it over the years, I realized that everything I held onto brewed inside of me, finally making its way to the surface when I got home. My relationships suffered tremendously, I began to feel like the makings of a mentally ill cat lady, destined to live a life alone.

The trips to the bathroom and missed meetings became more awkward as my disorder progressed. I lived in constant fear of being found out. My talents and abilities might be overlooked because of outbursts and mood swings. My blood shot eyes were mistaken for those of an alcoholic rather than a woman just trying to survive. I became terrified that my 75%, the problem solving and idea generating side of me, would never reach peak potential because of the 25% that haunted and undermined me.

The only thing I could do was lean into it and realize that my 25% was coming with me no matter what and we would graciously ride the waves of life as a unified force. No more apologies for skipping things during hell week and asking to be alone. No more guilt from the random thoughts that would take over my mind and no more hiding from myself and the world. I still had plenty to give and I was determined to live up to my fullest potential, 75% of the time. My 25% belonged to me, no one could take it from me, no one would mute the incredibly raw emotions that I was forced to confront every month, and no one would dare to ever use it against me. The woman in the basement was with me and she could error-correct along the way.

Three o'clock in the morning came too fast and eight AM couldn't come early enough. Closing my laptop for the night, I'd sleep for a few hours before getting up and doing it again. Checking in with the PMDD sub-reddit kept me focused. I knew that every day that passed was a missed opportunity to tell the world a story that everyone needed to hear, a story of compassion and self-love, a story about tragedy, a story about the other side of despair.

Every day there were women who felt like dying just for the week, and I made it a point to comment on their posts as much as possible and offer them the support they deserved. Line by line, their personal accounts of how they felt and the thoughts they had were eerily familiar. I felt connected in a way that strengthened and inspired me, giving me a sense of urgency and duty to offer them a new perspective on living with their 25%. And by lifting them up, I learned how to love myself in the process.

After so many years, I felt like I'd finally found out who I was, and I was starting to live as someone who didn't want to die. All along, I just needed to show myself another way, to redirect my attention to what *can* be. After all the dedication I put into crafting an improved version of myself, I now had to protect it at all costs. The information I allowed in to be processed had to first be vetted with a fine-tooth comb and validated. I'd ask for feedback from many but react to very few. In fact, I began to realize that reacting was not what I wanted to do. I wanted to inspire and provide hope, through action, not reaction.

One line from a stranger would give me goosebumps, and became the quote that I would hang on my wall and stare at every single day:

"This is simply amazing. I'm in tears right now, yet so inspired by you. Please keep writing."

(Mandeh M.)

When I shared my intro in the writing sub-reddit, I didn't expect much feedback, most aspiring writers were into fiction and fantasy not self-help books. I asked only two short questions: "What are your expectations for the next chapters?" and "Would you keep reading?"

The fact that my words could inspire someone I'd never met before was exhilarating, so electrifying, so unreal. The comment left me sitting on the edge of my bed and, pausing for a moment, I allowed the words to seep in. I could feel her keystrokes as she typed; without knowing, she programmed love songs into my soul. She wouldn't know for quite some time how her words inspired me to keep pushing, regardless of the challenges I would face as a first-time author.

Her comment came right on time, a few days after a different kind of feedback. A well-meaning friend asked me what my book was really about and reminded me that most self-help books are written by wildly successful people. Looking around at my tiny apartment, I still felt wildly successful. I felt like I'd overcome myself, I felt like I was just getting started. I saw the way, I had the vision, my mind was focused, and my intent was clear. I appreciated his candor because it was straight to the point: what if people don't read my book because I'm not their definition of success?

The next level version of myself was hardwired to validate information before it crept in, my work would be safeguarded at all costs. His comment was simply a matter of his own imagination, it wasn't meant to harm me, but the damage it might have caused had I let it take hold would have been the same regardless of intent. Locked into a state of self-awareness, without endless conversation and noise, I took plenty of time to analyze thoughts from others and myself before allowing them to access my self-worth. I did not internalize these negative thoughts and make them part of me. I mastered the art of input validation, effectively stopping any damaging thoughts from getting in.

I'd quarantine them, analyze them, and ask two simple questions to define their relevance: *does this thought serve me well* and *does this thought serve my book well?*

In computer programming, input validation is used to ensure that only proper data can be entered into a system, preventing malfunctions that may occur downstream. An example of this is when an online form is filled out, a box meant for numbers shouldn't allow text. Validation should occur as early in the process as possible and be strict with untrusted sources.

In my case, I learned how to build validators for all sources, especially myself during hell week. After rebuilding my system, I couldn't allow garbage data to disrupt my workflow and cause damage to myself or my work. My greatness wasn't up to me to define. That had already been defined by the Universe. My talents were already built into me and simply needed to be nurtured to bring them to the point of fulfilling my potential. So, my job was simply to protect, nurture, and allow that greatness to thrive. Fighting back against the ways of the world is futile; negativity will surround us even from trusted friends and family who mean well. It is up to us to build a feedback framework and allow positivity, even when it's seemingly in short supply, to radiate through us and provide us with the energy to keep going.

Looking back at my mom, she was never taught how to validate what was coming in from the world. The fact that she couldn't do math was irrelevant in the grand scheme of things. Despite her efforts, she still can't do math in her 50's and no one cares. What the world should care about, however, is that she stopped creating art for too many years.

My program was built on the preface that I would live my life to the fullest 75% of the time. Constructive criticism and enriching ideas would be allowed in so long as they offered value towards the goal. Negative thoughts would die a slow painful death at the hands of the woman in the basement, and she was good at her job.

"In the universe there is an immeasurable indescribable force which shamans call intent, and absolutely everything that exists in the entire cosmos is attached to intent by a connecting link."

(Carlos Castaneda)

ITERATIONS

"As you grow older, you will discover that you have two hands, one for helping yourself, the other for helping others."

(Maya Angelou)

2020 was a year of great change, a year of growth and triumph, it was the other side of my despair. It was the year that I found my calling, my passion in life. Feeling the sun on my skin, I finished the last words of this book on Memorial Day, a silent tribute to everyone who lost their lives so I could write. I thought about the soldiers who never returned, I thought about Gia. I thought about my future, living a life of purpose, living as the intentional version of myself. I thought about the generations of women before me, silently struggling to maintain composure through hell week.

I mourned for those we had already lost to this disorder, I mourned for their loved ones, many of whom still didn't have answers. I thought about our next generations of women and mourned those who would take their own lives before realizing their gifts. I grieved for the past version of myself as I laid her to rest, she was simply dealt a hand that she didn't know how to play. She endured a great deal of pain, her own biology plotted against her month after month silently stealing her thoughts, telling her that life wasn't worth living, that her own life had no value and that the only way to escape was to no longer exist.

But her struggles wouldn't be in vain, rather they would be a constant reminder of the power that we all have inside of us if we just listen closely enough. It had been six months since I met the woman in the basement, an experience that pulled me back from the constant cycle of negativity and changed my life for the better. She was a reminder of my own ability to change, to grow, to succeed. The method that introduced her into the world—my world—may be controversial for some, but for those of us who struggle immensely through the human condition, it may very well be the difference between life and death.

As the fuzziness began to creep up on me, the familiar feelings of emptiness and anger, depression, and anxiety, I knew it was time to reach out for her again. Feeling refreshed, I pulled the silk sheets from my skin and stepped out of bed and into the virtual corner of a dark basement. My hair fell to the small of my back, a few bouncing curls at the ends. Slipping on a tight black dress, the fabric felt smooth against my body, it fit just right and hugged all my curves. I stepped into my favorite heels and picked up a small book on the nightstand.

Moving across the room, I carefully studied the blue glowing lights of the server racks, tracing the cables with my hazel eyes. The glow was mesmerizing, the quiet hum of the equipment filled the room. Looking down at the book, I opened the first page and felt the goosebumps on my skin. Love songs began to play, and the silver linings of my femininity appeared front and center.

I felt whole, not because I was perfect, but because I knew that perfect didn't matter. Feeling ready, I moved to the bottom of the stairs. I was an incredibly happy woman, a nurturer, a caregiver, a life changer, and an advocate for sufferers of PMDD. All the time I spent writing was well worth it, the book was ready for others to enjoy now.

Each step was met with great intention as I reviewed each chapter. Remembering my uptime, I was devoted to being the absolute best version of myself 75% of the time. 25% of the time would be spent exclusively on self-care. I released any expectations of the next version of my life. It wasn't up to me to define my greatness; my only job was to allow the space for it to exist and thrive.

I had plenty of money to release my ideas into the world. Reaching for my retirement account, I had exactly $5,000 to invest. It was enough for an editor and a graphic designer to polish my work. I reminded myself that throughput was far more important than bandwidth and I could remove my limitations by driving on a road I created myself.

I rehearsed my values, remembering that I had to maintain self-awareness at all costs, I couldn't take the chance of losing my sense of self throughout the process. I promised that I wouldn't allow others to sway my writing, it was my own, a deep reflection of self that I found through solitude and individualism. Emerging into the world again required that I planned trips back to the basement often to recharge and find solace in being alone. I would never allow too much stimulation to weigh me down.

Preparing myself for change, I reminded myself that the world around me was never to be controlled. Strapping myself in for the ride, I was well suited for the emotional roller coaster of the next chapters of my life. I didn't need to see ahead, I just needed to make sure I was always ready to adapt. Feedback would come in various forms, some good, some bad, and some very ugly. This time around, my system was guarded like Fort Knox and only I had a key.

Approaching the top of the staircase, I found an infinite hallway lined with doors. Behind each one was an avenue, a path to put my ideas on display and pitch my book to others. Behind the first door was a group of people that I had met over the years, former managers, soldiers, and friends who saw something in me before I even saw it within myself. The boss who asked specifically for my brain when solving a problem met me with open arms. The Army sergeant who told me I was still a great soldier even though I cried a lot was standing in full uniform. The former coworker turned entrepreneur was typing at a computer, his simple comment about my higher frequency had come full circle. He felt my vibes early on and knew that my time spent working for others was limited. I didn't know what he meant until this moment.

Every single one of my friends were there, reminiscing about our time in the garage, telling jokes and playing loud music. My family was there, my mother filled with pride as she watched her daughter release her own version of art for the world to enjoy. My daughter and her father were there, laughing cheerfully together and cheering me on. His sister and his mother were there, greeting me at the door with hugs and wishing me well. My ex-husband, his family, and my son were there, supporting me from the sidelines.

Moving to the center of the room, I thanked them all for showing up, I thanked them for seeing through my 25% and for offering their kind words over the years. I explained to each and every one of them individually how they helped me at times that I couldn't help myself. I graciously asked them to read my book and tell the world what they thought. My heart filled with gratitude as they flipped open the pages and began to read.

Slipping on a white blazer over my black dress, I fixed my hair and took a deep breath. I entered the next door with my newfound sense of self. This room had more of a cocktail party feel, the vibe was vastly different. I had never met any of the people in this room. Like the last, each one of them had unknowingly inspired me with their words of wisdom. From my tiny apartment, I turned to them when I needed inspiration. Their stories of triumph and overcoming challenges pushed me to keep getting better. I couldn't bring myself to move to the center of this room, it was filled with too many powerful minds to address at one time.

Everyone here had found great success; they were all in and their greatness spilled over for millions to enjoy. Moving to the first table, I found Tim Ferriss. His book[11] *The 4 Hour Work Week* showed me that I didn't have to be confined to traditional work, I could carve out enough time for myself and find time to be unwell. I thanked him for his podcast, in particular the episodes on psilocybin and his partnership with Johns Hopkins Center for Psychedelics and Consciousness Research. I asked him to have his virtual assistant read my book and tell the world what he thought.

Daymond John was across the room in a perfectly tailored suit, and I pulled up a chair next to him. I thanked him for his book, *The Power of Broke*.[12] Reading his first-hand account of launching a successful business with no money provided me with a great deal of hope. There was dignity in the struggle, and he offered a set of silver linings to growing up without money that I could relate to. I asked him to read my book and offer suggestions on how I could hustle even harder; how I could get my book in front of more people without a marketing budget.

Next up was Joe Rogan, a wildly successful open-minded influencer.[13] He was a male role model with a vast audience of men of all ages. I asked him to help me explain the disorder to men. Sufferers tend to hide female problems from their partners, their fathers, and their male friends, coworkers, and bosses. Not knowing how to talk to them about it caused an extra layer of stress that I thought could be avoided. I asked him to talk about menstruation and mushrooms, because if anyone could pull it off it was him.

My next table was the most nerve wracking. I pulled myself together and sat down next to Shonda Rhimes, the female titan responsible for creating the hit series *Grey's Anatomy* and *Scandal* was one of my biggest motivators. I thanked her for paving the way for more women, for her TED Talk[14] on always saying yes despite fear. I thanked her for her definition of the *hum*, an addicting feeling when you're in the zone and living up to your absolute potential. I asked her to read my book, I asked her to read about my version of the hum.

My time in this room was bold, but I knew that their ideas of a life well lived were similar to mine. They too, found their own calling and reached down to help others up, perpetuating their own cycle of success.

Moving to the next room, I took a moment to ground myself before entering. This room was quite different from the last but was the most important to my work. A diverse group of women, some young, some old, coming from all walks of life, some suffering and some not. Moving towards the center of this room felt ritualistic. It was as if I was asking for acceptance from a higher power, something much bigger than myself.

The room of sufferers were members of a unique tribe of women, many of whom stayed hidden from the world. The unwritten rules were as prevalent here as they were in our online forums, always be kind, never judge, and always lift each other up. My interactions with the group were pleasant 100% of the time, even during hell week. The forums filled with first-hand accounts of suicidal thoughts and feelings of hopelessness. Posts never went unanswered for more than an hour, as women from all over jumped in to help, offering support to complete strangers.

We had a different way of living than most, and the words in my book would expose our strengths and weaknesses to the world. The fact that we were all still standing was a modern-day miracle and we all knew it. I asked them to read my book and I asked them for their acceptance of my work. I asked them with the utmost respect, knowing that I was telling a secret that so many of them tried to hide. And I asked them with the greatest personal respect, knowing what each of them had endured. I offered a copy to one woman in particular, a sufferer herself who endured the added nightmare of losing her beautiful daughter Gia to PMDD. I offered my condolences for her loss and told her about the impact her story had on my life.

Putting myself on display for the world to see is something I never imagined I would do. Realizing how much we all have in common; I knew that my experiences could help others through their own moments of despair.

Expectations from the world were long gone, I felt a sense of duty and service to keep going despite uncertainty and not being able to see the next step. The way I grew up was out of my control, and the idea that I was destined for less was simply a manifestation of my environment and imagination. Had I grown up in a family of successful writers, I never would have questioned my ability and passion. Focusing on throughput instead of bandwidth, I removed the handcuffs of my disorder. My values guided me. Staying in tune with who I was at all times was the very mechanism that helped me navigate the challenges of my own mind. If I could remain grounded, my switch in thoughts, feelings, and emotions would never push me off course. With my feet planted firmly on the earth I could withstand the changing of my own seasons.

PMDD brought plenty of hardship, but it also offered unique silver linings. My brain chemistry changes every month, but through the changes I learned how to master the art of mind control.

I learned that our thoughts are not always our own, but the constant replaying of everything we've ever seen, read, heard, or been told. I learned that our self-talk is the most powerful and we must get quiet enough to listen to the woman in the basement, the woman screaming to be unleashed into world with all her vulnerabilities exposed.

I learned that in order to take control of my life, I had to replace those old thoughts, which no longer served me, with new ones, thoughts that told me I was right, I was capable, and I was talented.

Everything we pull in must first be quarantined and studied for usefulness or lack of value to our personal circumstance.

I learned that we must develop our own system of intention, something that's meaningful to us, something that we can understand and apply.

The best tools are the ones that work, and if we can't find the right ones, we can create them ourselves. After the building, the tinkering, the fixing, the creating, we finally take a step back and realize that the work was the gift all along.

"When the voice and vision on the inside become more profound and clear and loud than the opinions on the outside, you've mastered your life."
(Dr. John Demartini)

There is no definition of done, we don't reach the peak and stop climbing. When we finally reach the top, we simply turn around to show others the way, lifting them up to walk alongside us.

ABOUT THE AUTHOR

Tina Williams is a longtime sufferer of premenstrual dysphoric disorder, otherwise known as PMDD. Her journey through life with an undiagnosed mood disorder offers unique self-development perspectives and alternative ways of approaching women's mental health issues.

Before her diagnosis, she earned a master's in information systems and navigated the world of the hi-tech industry, studying systems and how components interact with one another. She loves to travel with her two children and go on long runs with her dog Lucky.

To find out more about Tina, visit her website: womaninthebasement.com

REFERENCES

1. Staff. "About PMDD." International Association for Premenstrual Disorders, March 2019
   https://iapmd.org/facts-and-figures

2. Dubey, Neelima, et al. "The EXC/E(Z) complex, an effector of response to ovarian steroids, manifests an intrinsic difference in cells from women with Premenstrual Dysphoric Disorder." PubMedCentral (PMC). NCBI, Jan 2017
   https://www.ncbi.nlm.nih.gov/pmc/articles/PMC5495630/

3. Carhart-Harris, Robin L. and Goodwin, Guy M. "The Therapeutic Potential of Psychedelic Drugs: Past, Present, and Future." PubMedCentral (PMC). NCBI, May 2017.
   https://www.ncbi.nlm.nih.gov/pmc/articles/PMC5603818/#bib79

4. Murray, Jon. "Denver first in U.S. to decriminalize psychedelic mushrooms." The Denver Post. Media News Group, Inc., May 2019.
   https://www.denverpost.com/2019/05/08/denver-psychedelic-magic-mushroom/

5. Griffiths, Roland. "The science of psilocybin and its use to relieve suffering." YouTube. TEDMED, Nov. 2015.
   https://www.youtube.com/watch?v=81-v8ePXPd4#action=share

6. Mason, N.L., et al. "Me, myself, bye: regional alterations in glutamate and the experience of ego dissolution with psilocybin." Nature Research. Neuropsychopharmacology, May 2020.
   https://www.nature.com/articles/s41386-020-0718-8#Sec8

7. Ly, Calvin, et al. "Psychedelics Promote Structural and Functional Neural Plasticity." PubMedCentral (PMC). NCBI, Aug 2018.
https://www.ncbi.nlm.nih.gov/pmc/articles/PMC6082376/

8. Raines, Deborah A. and Cooper, Danielle B. "Braxton Hicks Contractions." StatPearls. NCBI, April 2020.
https://www.google.com/search?q=waht+are+braxton+hicks+contracti
ons&oq=waht+are+braxton+hicks+contractions&aqs=chrome..69i57j0l7.56
25j0j7&sourceid=chrome&ie=UTF-8

9. Chisholm, Andrea MD. "Premenstrual dysphoria disorder: It's biology, not a behavior choice." Harvard Health Publishing. Harvard Medical School, May 2017.
https://www.health.harvard.edu/blog/premenstrual-dysphoria-disorder-
its-biology-not-a-behavior-choice-2017053011768

10. Staff. *2019 National Veteran Suicide Prevention Annual Report.* U.S. Department of Veterans Affairs. 2019
https://www.mentalhealth.va.gov/docs/data-
sheets/2019/2019_National_Veteran_Suicide_Prevention_Annual_Report_
508.pdf

11. Ferriss, Timothy. *The 4 Hour Work Week: Escape 9-5, Live Anywhere, and Join the New Rich.* New York: Random House, Inc., 2009

12. John, Daymond. *The Power of Broke: How Empty Pockets, A Tight Budget, and a Hunger for Success Can Become Your Greatest Competitive Advantage.* New York: Penguin Random House LLC, 2016

13. Staff. "Joe Rogan Biography." International Movie Database (IMDb). Accessed June 6, 2020

14. Rhimes, Shonda. "My year of saying yes to everything." YouTube. TED, Feb. 2016.

15. Griffiths, Roland, Psilocybin produces substantial and sustained decreases in depression and anxiety in patients with life-threatening cancer: A randomized double-blind trial. Journal of Psychopharmacology, 2016.

Made in the USA
Las Vegas, NV
24 March 2021